FINANCIAL STATEMENTS
FOR
NON-FINANCIAL
PEOPLE

A Quick-and-Easy Guide to
Reading a Financial Statement

R O N P R I C E , M . B . A .

Adams Media
Avon, Massachusetts

Published by
Adams Media, an F+W Publications Company
57 Littlefield Street, Avon, MA 02322. U.S.A.
www.adamsmedia.com

ISBN: 1-58062-946-6

Printed in the United States of America.

J I H G F E D C B A

Library of Congress Cataloging-in-Publication Data
Price, Ron
Financial statements for non-financial people / Ron Price.
p.   cm.
ISBN 1-58062-946-6
1. Financial statements. I. Title.

HF5681.B2P74 2003
332.63'2042--dc21
                              2003004475

This publication is designed to provide accurate and authoritative information with regard to
the subject matter covered. It is sold with the understanding that the publisher is not engaged
in rendering legal, accounting, or other professional advice. If legal advice or other expert
assistance is required, the services of a competent professional person should be sought.
—From a *Declaration of Principles* jointly adopted by a Committee of the American Bar
Association and a Committee of Publishers and Associations

Many of the designations used by manufacturers and sellers to distinguish their products
are claimed as trademarks. Where those designations appear in this book and Adams
Media was aware of a trademark claim, the designations have been printed with initial
capital letters.

Special thanks to Michelle Cagan, C.P.A.,
for her technical review of the manuscript.

*This book is available at quantity discounts for bulk purchases.
For information, call 1-800-872-5627.*

Contents

Dedication

To my past, present, and future students—in whose hands our financial future may rest, as simultaneously encouraging and frightful as that may be.

Acknowledgments

I'd like to acknowledge: the teachers, instructors, and professors who earnestly endeavored to teach finance and economics to me; the accountants, lawyers, entrepreneurs, and consultants with whom I've worked over the years, who gave me the real skinny on financial matters; and to the fine folks at Adams Media for giving me a forum in which to express my tangential points of view.

Introduction

I take some pride in the fact that my business students can, after overcoming their inherent fears, read, analyze, and understand financial statements. I am writing this book to provide a service to humanity by debunking the myths and mystery that for some reason surround financial statements, annual reports, or whatever you like to call them.

A number of myths and urban legends have grown concerning financial statements. To some people, financial statements are proof of extraterrestrial life on earth and that financial statements are the encoded secret messages of these creatures from outer space that are obviously plotting to overthrow life as we know it. Another myth is that financial statements require a great deal of complicated mathematics to understand. Yet another says that you can only understand a financial statement if you wear pinstripes, suspenders, and wire-rimmed glasses and talk real fast. I've been told that even holding a company's annual report can cause normal people to break out in a cold sweat and blur their vision. And no, reading Proust is not easier than reading a financial statement.

Be that as it may, financial statements are none of this and certainly nothing to fear. In fact, financial statements are actually only organized accounting reports published periodically by corporations.

Okay, so I invoked the "A" word—*accounting*, which always means mystery and deception, doesn't it? Perhaps, but if you understand that all of the accountant's magic and sleight-of-hand is behind the scenes and that all you have to deal with on the financial statement is only the set of final numbers they cranked out, then you will see through this supposed deception.

Also understand that financial reports aren't necessarily put out voluntarily. Several government agencies, primarily the Securities Exchange Commission (SEC), and those fun-loving people at banks and stock brokerage houses require—no demand—financial statements from any corporation with publicly traded stock. So, reading and understanding financial statements is actually a blow for the common person against the evil empire of big business and their accounting sorcerers.

Okay, but there is no gain without some pain. I know it may sound like a contradiction, but "reading" financial statements really means analyzing them. Only by pairing, contrasting, and comparing the amounts published in the statements can you "read" the reports and gain an understanding of what the numbers are truly saying. As the proverb has it, the devil is truly in the details. So, it is my goal in this book to provide you with the analysis tools you can use to dig out the real story about how good or bad a company is doing.

Companies do their best to make their financial statements look as good as they can with pictures of the management team, a glowing letter from the CEO, and a very supportive letter from their accountants. While these make interesting and on occasion humorous reading, it's the numbers and the notes explaining why each number is not so bad and how it will be better in the future that truly provide the information you seek.

So, without trying to sound too much like an accountant, trust me and together we can chase away the aliens and debunk the myths surrounding these truly informative and valuable documents.

Part 1

Introduction

Reading a financial statement can be confusing and a bit intimidating to anyone who doesn't know its language and what its numbers truly mean. This part of the book provides a brief introduction and overview of a company's annual report with a focus on its financial statements.

Chapter 1

Keeping Score

*A financial statement is a scorecard and
like any scorecard, it shows results.*

Reporting the Score

I don't know if you are a baseball fan or not (please excuse the sports metaphor if you aren't), but the final score of a baseball game really doesn't tell you much about what actually happened in the game. To really understand more about how each of the players performed and how the game progressed, you need to study the game's box score. The box score provides you with as much of an understanding as you can get without actually attending, watching, or listening to the game. Studying the statistics and summaries of a baseball game's box score helps you to "*see*" the game in retrospect.

Likewise, just knowing that a corporation had a profit or loss doesn't tell you the whole story about the corporation and its operations. You need something like a box score or a scorecard to gain an insight into how the corporation is performing and reaching its results. This is where financial statements come in.

A Snapshot in Time

A corporation's financial statements provide insight into a corporation's financial status at a given point in time. In most cases these statements are produced at the end of the corporation's fiscal year, which can run the calendar year (January to December) or any 12-month period, such as July to June, October to September, or April to March. Each financial statement is a snapshot of the corporation's finances taken exactly at the end of the fiscal period. Like the baseball box score, financial statements help us to understand the final results of the corporation at the end of the "game"—its fiscal year.

Financial statements freeze in time a corporation's financial information. Just as it is hard to hit a moving target, trying to measure an enterprise's health and well-being on the fly would be difficult at best. Only by freeze-framing the numbers that report where a corporation is in terms of its assets, liabilities, income, expenses, and other financial categories are we able to determine how well the corporation is doing.

Umpires and Auditors

Of course, whether in a baseball game or in financial accounting, we know that, unfortunately, there are bound to be cheaters. Recent corporate events have borne this out. In a baseball game, umpires are used to make judgments on balls and strikes and safe and out, and to keep the game fair and impartial.

When it comes to financial records though, public accounting firms (and their hordes of certified public accountants [CPAs]) audit a corporation's financial records to determine if the generally accepted accounting practices (commonly known as GAAP) are being followed and that the numbers presented by the enterprise have validity. At the risk of oversimplifying what a public accountant does, the CPA, like the baseball umpire, makes the "safe" and "out" calls on a corporation's financial records.

Not every enterprise is required to use an official "umpire" though. Private corporations, partnerships, and sole proprietorships are not technically required to produce financial statements for public review. Therefore, they are not legally bound to have their financial records and practices reviewed by an independent auditor. Although a few of these companies do go to the expense of having their records and practices reviewed, reliance on their financial statements is a matter of faith. We'll take a deeper look into who is required (and who is not required) to produce audited statements later in the book.

Good Times/Bad Times

One of my college professors once told the class that you can very easily tell whether a corporation has had a good year or a bad year. He said that if a company has color pictures of its executives in the financial reports, it was a good year. In a bad year, if there are any pictures at all, they are black and white. If only making a good/bad determination was really this easy.

The Devil Is in the Details

While there may be some truth (mostly coincidence, I think) to this theory, in reality, it isn't a matter of pictures or their color. Only through a careful reading and analysis of at least one year of a corporation's financial statements are you able to develop reliable information on which to make a good year/bad year determination. And, in the end, you are the ultimate judge on how well or poorly a corporation may have done.

Financial statements aren't the sorts you'd take to the beach for some light summer reading, at least not in my opinion anyway. Typically, you would study a corporation's financial statements because you either have or are considering an investment in the corporation. Perhaps the primary reason the average person, as opposed to an investment banker, stock analyst, or financial underwriter, would study a corporation's financial statements is to decide whether or not to buy or sell the company's stocks and bonds. In addition, the employees of any corporation have perhaps the best reason to study their company's financial statements: to know how well their employer is doing and how it relates to their job. In far too many situations, the employees of a corporation rarely even pick up their employer's financial statements, let alone read or study them, even in situations where the corporation's stock is the foundation of their retirement funds.

Digging out the Details

The focus of this book is to provide you with the information and processes used to make such a judgment. The process is not overly complicated, taken one step at a time, but you must be able to dig out the details needed. Each of the various financial statements tells its own tale and knowing how to read and interpret the data is the key to understanding the tale it tells.

In the following sections of this chapter, I will provide you with an overview of each of the more common financial statements: the Balance Sheet, the Income Statement, and the Cash Flow Statement (also known as the Sources and Uses of Funds Statement). The first step to understanding what each statement has to report is understanding exactly what each statement includes and its purpose.

Who Must Publish Financial Statements (and Why)

All U.S. companies with more than 500 investors and $10 million in net assets and all companies that list their stocks with a major national stock exchange, such as the New York Stock Exchange, the American Stock Exchange, or the NASDAQ stock market, must register with the SEC and file annual reports, which include financial statements, with the SEC.

However, there are companies that don't have to register or file with the SEC. A company that raises $5 million of investor money in a 12-month period can be exempted from filing under the SEC's

Regulation A. Small companies that raise less than $1 million in one year from stock offerings aren't required to register with the SEC (under Regulation D, Section 504).

You can view the annual reports filed by the SEC's registered companies for free by visiting the SEC's EDGAR database at ✍*www.sec.gov/edgar.shtml.*

Most publicly traded companies (those who offer their stock to the general public, rather than offering it only to internal investors) compile and publish an annual report for their shareholders. However, many companies are privately held, which means their stock is not available to the public, and aren't required to publish their financial statements, which many don't. Some not-for-profit organizations (non-profits) publish publicly available financial statements, and then some don't.

It is likely that if you are interested in looking over a company's financial statements, you wish to invest in it, go to work for it, or both. If the company is a publicly traded corporation and one you may wish to buy stock in, chances are that its financial statements can be obtained either from the SEC, a library, or a stock evaluation company, like Morningstar (✍*www.morningstar.com*).

The Annual Report

A company's annual report, the kind required by the SEC and specified by the Financial Accounting Standards Board (FASB), contains more than just its financial statements. An annual report is an opportunity for a company to make their case to investors, lenders, and even to existing and potential future employees.

By and large, the contents of a company's annual report varies a bit with its industry, its recent performance (good or bad), and the message the company wishes to send. However, nearly all annual reports contain a set of required and customary elements, including:

CHAIRPERSON'S REPORT: A report from the chairperson of the board (COB) or the chief executive officer (CEO) that provides a summary of the past year and typically an explanation of where the company is headed. Some annual reports may have a report from both the COB and the CEO.

AUDITOR'S REPORT: If the company issuing the annual report is a publicly traded corporation, it is required to include an auditor's report. This report, commonly called an accountant's opinion, provides either a qualified or an unqualified opinion of the credibility, reliability, security, and accuracy of the records, processes, and procedures on which the financial statements are based. A qualified opinion means that the auditor found issues that it is required to disclose. An unqualified opinion means that the financial statements reasonably represent the company's financial status for the stated time period. The auditing accountant is typically a regional, national, or international public accounting firm, and the report is normally signed with the accounting firm's name by one of its partners or principals.

FINANCIAL STATEMENTS: A required part of an annual report are the company's financial statements, which at minimum must include a balance sheet, income statement, and a statement of cash flows. Additional reports may be included, such as a retained earnings statement, or other statements commonly used by a particular industry. Very large, multinational, or multi-company corporations typically produce consolidated statements summarizing the financial data of the entire corporation, leaving the detailed financial statements to the annual reports of each subsidiary company or business segment. In most cases, the statements include comparisons to at least the prior year and often more, which is handy for performing year-to-year comparisons and growth analysis on the company's data.

NOTES TO THE FINANCIAL STATEMENTS: Virtually all financial statements have notes, or explanatory or supplemental information, to explain the accounting methods used or special circumstances surrounding a particular entry. It is a very good idea to read the notes on a company's financial statement before beginning any analysis.

ORGANIZATION: Companies often include an organization chart or brief background statements and photographs of their key management personnel and their board of directors members in an effort to deinstitutionalize the corporation and give it a human face.

MISCELLANEOUS: A company can include just about anything it wishes in its financial report, especially if it helps those reading the reports gain a better understanding of the company's mission, vision, and future. You may see such things as a multi-year summary of its financials, an overview of its business competencies and expertise, and a statement of where the company sees itself heading in the future. Some companies even include the minutes of their latest shareholders' meetings.

The Big Three in Financial Statements

The primary financial statements included in a company's annual report are its balance sheet, income statement, and statement of cash flows. These three reports are the focus of this book. In the chapters that follow, the contents of each of these three financial statements are looked at in detail, and information on how to go about interpreting the information they contain is provided.

However, just to get started, let's take a quick look at each of these statements and their purpose, format, and contents. The following sections do just that.

The Balance Sheet

The philosophy behind the balance sheet financial report is that a company's assets must balance to (equal) its liabilities and its owners' or shareholders' equity, hence the name. **TABLE 1-1** shows a sample balance sheet.

Note: The balance sheet in **TABLE 1-1** is for a fictitious company, as are all of the financial reports and simulated records included in this book. Any resemblance to any company, thriving, squeaking by, or belly up, is strictly coincidental.

TABLE 1-1: A SAMPLE BALANCE SHEET

Dogs on the Run, Inc.
Balance Sheet December 31, 2002

Assets	
Current assets	
Cash	$10,000
Accounts receivable	$2,000
Inventory	$5,000
Total current assets	$17,000
Fixed assets	
Equipment	$82,000
Buildings	$73,000
(Less depreciation)	$(12,000)
Total fixed assets	$143,000
Intangible assets	$5,000
Total assets	$165,000
Liabilities and shareholders' equity	
Liabilities	
Current liabilities	
Accounts payable	$5,000

Taxes payable	$7,000
Total current liabilities	$12,000
Long-term liabilities	
Long-term loans	$60,000
Total liabilities	$72,000
Shareholders' equity	
Common stock	$80,000
Retained earnings	$13,000
Total shareholders' equity	$93,000
Total liabilities and shareholders' equity	$165,000

When a company purchases any asset (see "Assets" later in the chapter), it must either pay for it from its existing assets, create a liability, or draw on its shareholders' equity. If a company purchases a $10,000 asset, it must pay out $10,000 from its cash or cash equivalents or borrow funds and create a $10,000 liability entry.

If $10,000 in cash is used to pay for the asset, cash assets are reduced by $10,000 and fixed assets are increased by $10,000, which has no effect on the total assets amount. However, if the asset is purchased on credit, its $10,000 value is added to assets and a matching $10,000 entry is added to the company's liabilities, increasing both sides of the balance sheet.

Generally, a corporation would not dip into its retained earnings or issue new stock to raise only $10,000. Anyway, the idea is that assets must equal liabilities and shareholders' equity at all times, which is the balance sheet's identity.

What's on a Balance Sheet?

Beyond assets, liabilities, and shareholders' equity, there isn't very much in the way of extra information to behold on a balance sheet. The fact that the balance sheet balances is of primary interest (and I doubt you'd ever see a published balance sheet that was out

of balance). Beyond that, the information is in the individual numbers and their relationships with one another (see Chapter 3).

Let's take a very quick look at the contents of a balance sheet.

Assets

Assets are tangible and intangible property that carry value in a
transaction and can be used to accomplish a company's primary
mission. A company's mission will normally have something to do
with producing a product or service, selling the product or service,
and generating the most possible profit. The assets of a company are
applied to help a company achieve its mission or goals.

Tangible properties are things that have a physical presence.
Tangible assets are properties that can be touched, seen, smelled,
and even heard, such as buildings, machinery, cars, trucks, computers (some of which even speak), and the like. Tangible assets all
have value, which is typically set by their purchase prices.

Intangible properties do not have physical presence and cannot
be seen, touched, or anything. Intangible assets are things like intellectual properties, trademarks, copyrights, patents, and goodwill.
Okay, so you can see a trademark or a patented piece of equipment,
but what creates the value of an intangible asset is not a thing, it's
more of a what—the copyright, the patent, and the goodwill of a
company's customers. The financial measurement of an intangible
asset is somewhat subjective because it's usually based on a per-
ceived value rather than a purchase price.

Categories and Classes of Assets

Assets are either current or long-term. A current asset is one that
is cash or can become cash in less than one business cycle of a company or one year, whichever is longer. A business cycle is the length
of time required to produce or acquire a product, sell that product to
a customer and receive payment from the customer, and not a
motorized two-wheeled vehicle used only in business. Business

cycles can run from two weeks to two years depending on the business, its industry, and its products. **TABLE 1-2** shows the current assets portion of a balance sheet.

The current asset that draws the most attention is cash. Cash includes currency, coins, and demand deposits (checking accounts). Near-cash, which is also referred to as cash equivalents, includes short-term securities, such as bearer bonds, money-market accounts, and certificates of deposit (CDs).

A long-term asset is one that cannot be converted into cash within a single business cycle and has a service life of at least three years. Some long-term assets are also referred to as fixed assets. **TABLE 1-3** shows the long-term assets portion of a balance sheet.

TABLE 1-2: THE CURRENT ASSETS PORTION OF A BALANCE SHEET

Assets	
Current assets	
Cash	$10,000
Accounts receivable	$2,000
Inventory	$5,000
Total current assets	$17,000

TABLE 1-3: THE LONG-TERM ASSETS PORTION OF A BALANCE SHEET

Long-term assets	
Fixed assets	
Equipment	$82,000
Buildings	$73,000
(Less depreciation)	$(12,000)
Total fixed assets	$143,000
Intangible assets	$5,000

The overall value of long-term assets is usually adjusted during their service lives to reflect the portion of their original value that has been consumed or has been deflated with age.

Liabilities

In general, a company's liabilities are its debts. Just like we all have bills to pay each month, quarter, and year, so do corporations. Like assets, liabilities can be either short-term or long-term, but the distinction for liabilities has to do with when they will be paid. A liability that will come due and be paid within the next year is a short-term liability, which is more commonly referred to as a current liability. Examples of current liabilities are accounts payable, interest payments, and income taxes yet to be paid. **TABLE 1-4** shows the current liabilities portion of a balance sheet.

TABLE 1-4: THE CURRENT LIABILITIES
PORTION OF A BALANCE SHEET

Current liabilities	
Accounts payable	$5,000
Taxes payable	$7,000
Total current liabilities	$12,000

Long-term liabilities are those liabilities that are neither due nor will be paid within the next year. **TABLE 1-5** displays long-term liabilities, which include a company's longer-range obligations, such as bank loans, notes, and bonds issued by the company.

TABLE 1-5: THE LONG-TERM LIABILITIES
PORTION OF A BALANCE SHEET

Long-term liabilities	
Long-term loans	$60,000

Shareholders' Equity

There are two primary entries included in the shareholders' equity portion of a corporate balance sheet: retained earnings and the value of a company's common stock, as shown in **TABLE 1-6**. Other accounts that may be included in the equity section of the balance sheet include treasury stock (a company's own stock that it has bought back from investors) and paid-in capital (the value of the owners' original contribution over and above the stated par value of the stock).

TABLE 1-6: THE SHAREHOLDERS' EQUITY
PORTION OF A BALANCE SHEET

Shareholders' equity	
Common stock	$80,000
Retained earnings	$13,000
Total shareholders' equity	$93,000

The common stock entry, shown in **TABLE 1-6**, represents the book value, as opposed to the market value, of any shares a company has issued. In addition, the shareholders' equity section of the balance sheet includes the balance of the retained earnings account. Retained earnings represent the accumulation of the amounts of net income (or losses) that have been retained by the company in lieu of paying out dividends to its shareholders.

Note: The term *shareholders' equity* (rather than *owners' equity*) should be used only when discussing publicly traded corporations. The term owners' equity is better used with privately held companies, like proprietorships and partnerships.

It is common for a company to show any distributions made to shareholders as dividends or any amount added to retained earnings in the reported year, so that the net income on the income statement is accounted for on the balance sheet.

Balancing the Balance Sheet

As I said earlier, the identity of the balance sheet is that the asset total must equal the total of liabilities and shareholders' equity, using the following formula:

Assets = Liabilities + Shareholders' equity

The Income Statement

The second of the big three financial statements in a company's annual report is the income statement. The income statement reports a company's performance in generating a profit by netting earnings to expenses. **TABLE 1-7** shows a sample income statement.

An income statement has three primary sections: revenues (earnings), cost of sales (cost of goods sold), and operating expenses and taxes. Chapter 4 provides much more detail on the income statement, but the next few sections provide an overview of the sections of the income statement.

TABLE 1-7: A SAMPLE INCOME STATEMENT

Dogs on the Run, Inc.
Income Statement for the Year Ended December 31, 2002

Revenues	
Wholesale sales	$140,432
Retail sales	$46,175
Gross revenues	$186,607
Cost of sales	
Food costs	$79,777
Other direct costs	$39,889
Total cost of sales	$119,666

Gross profit	$66,941
Operating expenses	
Selling and administrative expenses	$7,978
Depreciation	$4,600
Total operating expenses	$12,578
Operating income	$54,363
Interest expense	$2,375
Income before taxes	$51,988
Income taxes	$9,355
Net income	$42,633

Revenues (Earnings)

As shown in **TABLE 1-8**, the revenues or earnings section of an income statement reports the sources of a company's revenues for the reporting period and its total revenues.

TABLE 1-8: THE REVENUES SECTION OF AN INCOME STATEMENT

Revenues	
Wholesale sales	$140,432
Retail sales	$46,175
Gross revenues	$186,607

Typically the revenue numbers reported in the income statement are net amounts, which means that any adjustments to sales and other sources of income (from operations) are already taken out. Adjustments to revenues are things like customer discounts and returned goods. If the adjustments are significant enough, they may be listed separately on the income statement as a deducted amount.

Cost of Sales (Cost of Goods Sold)

Unless a company provides strictly professional services, such as advertising, marketing, medical services, accounting services, legal services, or the like, it incurs costs in producing or purchasing its products. The costs of raw materials, labor, overhead, and goods bought for resale, which are the costs of producing an income, are deducted to compute a company's gross profit. **TABLE 1-9** shows the cost of sales portion of an income statement.

TABLE 1-9: THE COST OF SALES PORTION OF AN INCOME STATEMENT

Cost of sales	
Food costs	$79,777
Other direct costs	$39,889
Total cost of sales	$119,666

The costs included in the cost of sales portion of an income statement are those incurred to produce, purchase, package, and ship products for customers. Every business exists to provide a product or service it sells to customers, hopefully at a profit.

In addition to the direct costs of producing a product, companies typically have other operating expenses that should be deducted from revenues, such as office supplies, utilities, and the like. And virtually every company of any size has depreciation expenses it deducts to account for the aging of its production facilities, equipment, and machinery.

Gross Profit

The net of revenues and costs of sales is gross profit. The gross profit, or gross income, amount is an indicator of several facets of a company's operations and management policies, including pricing, cost management, and its sales function.

Operating Income

The net of gross profit and operating expenses is operating income. Operating income, see **TABLE 1-10**, is the net amount after cost of sales and regular operating expenses are deducted from the revenues generated from customers purchasing a company's products or services. Operating income is not the bottom line, however, because some indirect expenses, like interest and income taxes, have yet to be deducted. In effect, operating income is a company's earnings minus the normal costs of conducting its business. However, operating income doesn't account for other activities, such as income from asset sales. Although it may seem odd, a company that has a negative operating income could still generate a positive bottom-line net income; for example, a company showing a net operating loss could sell off some large assets at a profit, and that profit could be greater than the operating loss, resulting in overall net income.

TABLE 1-10: THE OPERATING INCOME PORTION OF AN INCOME STATEMENT

Gross profit	$66,941
Operating expenses	
Selling and administrative expenses	$7,978
Depreciation	$4,600
Total operating expenses	$12,578
Operating income	$54,363

Indirect Expenses

The two primary categories of indirect expenses are interest and taxes, as shown in **TABLE 1-11**. Interest payments, which are charged on any money a company has borrowed, are deducted to yield a company's taxable income, or what is called its net income before taxes (NBT). From that figure, the income tax amount for the year is deducted, resulting in net income.

TABLE 1-11: THE INDIRECT EXPENSES
PORTION OF AN INCOME STATEMENT

Operating income	$54,363
Interest expense	<u>$2,375</u>
Income before taxes	$51,988
Income taxes	<u>$9,355</u>
Net income	$42,633

Net Income

As shown in **TABLE 1-11**, the bottom-line of an income state-ment is net income and it is, well, the bottom line. Net income is the profit amount a company has available to reinvest in the busi-ness (as retained earnings), distribute to its shareholders as divi-dends, or both.

Comprehensive Income

Many larger companies may include an additional section on their income statements—comprehensive income, which states the change in equity (or net assets) of the company from its regular transactions and other non-operating activities, such as foreign cur-rency conversion adjustments. The comprehensive income section lists any adjustments to net income and nets them to a comprehen-sive income amount.

Any out-of-the-ordinary happenings, like losses incurred because of hurricane damage or the closing of a large manufacturing plant, are indicated separately after the net income line. Changes to net income from extraordinary events (like the hurricane) or discon-tinued operations (like the plant closing) aren't really part of the day-to-day operations and aren't expected to happen on a regular basis. Because of their unusual nature, they are reported separately so readers of the financial statements can differentiate between true net income and that due to abnormal circumstances.

Cash Flows Statement

The cash flows statement goes by several names, including statement of cash flows and statement of changes in financial position, but I prefer cash flows statement, which is the one that is most commonly used. A sample cash flows statement (prepared using the indirect method) is included in **TABLE 1-12**.

The cash flows statement is a reconciliation of the changes that have occurred during the reported year to the amounts on the balance sheet and income statement, showing the cash inflows and outflows that created the changes.

A cash flows statement is divided into three sections:

- Cash flows from operating activities
- Cash flows from investing activities
- Cash flows from financing activities

The cash flows statement is discussed in detail in Chapter 6.

TABLE 1-12: A SAMPLE CASH FLOWS STATEMENT

Dogs on the Run, Inc.
Cash Flows Statement for the Year Ending 12/31/02

Cash flow from operating activities	
Net income	$42,633
Depreciation expense	$4,600
Increase in accounts receivable	$(1,200)
Increase in inventory	$(3,500)
Decrease in accounts payable	$(4,403)
Decrease in income taxes payable	$(12,500)
Total cash flow from operating activities	$25,630

**TABLE 1-12: A SAMPLE CASH FLOWS
STATEMENT (CONTINUED)**

Dogs on the Run, Inc.
Cash Flows Statement For The Year Ending 12/31/02

Cash flow from investing activities	
Purchase of property and equipment	$(25,000)
Total cash flow from investing activities	$(25,000)
Cash flow from financing activities	
Increase in long-term debt	$10,000
Capital stock issued	$2,000
Dividend payments	$(4,000)
Total cash flow from financing activities	$8,000
Net increase in cash	$8,630
Cash at beginning of year	$1,370
Cash at end of year	$10,000

Cash Flows from Operating Activities

The amounts shown in the cash flows from operating activities (see **TABLE 1-13**), which is also called the cash flows from operations or the operating cash flows on some statements, reflects the cash inflows and outflows that occurred during the reporting period from a company's normal operating activities. These cash flows represent the money a company received or spent to make, sell, ship, and administer products and services, which are its primary business.

TABLE 1-13: THE CASH FLOW FROM OPERATIONS PORTION OF A CASH FLOWS STATEMENT

Cash flow from operating activities	
Net income	$42,633
Depreciation expense	$4,600
Increase in accounts receivable	$(1,200)
Increase in inventory	$(3,500)
Decrease in accounts payable	$(4,403)
Decrease in income taxes payable	$(12,500)
Total cash flow from operating activities	$25,630

As we will discuss in later chapters, the total operating cash flow amount is a key amount to a number of tools used to analyze a company's performance. Because no matter how great a company's income statement looks, if the company isn't generating any cash, it will likely go out of business.

Cash Flows from Investing Activities

If during the reporting period a company invested in (purchased or improved) or sold buildings, equipment, machinery, computers, office furniture, and the like, it had cash flows in or out from these activities. These cash flows, typically reflected on the balance sheet, are reported in this section of the cash flows statement (see **TABLE 1-14**).

TABLE 1-14: THE CASH FLOW FROM INVESTING ACTIVITIES SECTION OF A CASH FLOWS STATEMENT

Cash flow from investing activities	
Purchase of property and equipment	$(25,000)
Total cash flow from investing activities	$(25,000)

Cash Flows from Financing Activities

Virtually all companies borrow money to expand, support, or sustain their operating or investing activities, which creates cash inflows and outflows for borrowed or invested funds. The alternative to borrowing in these circumstances is selling an interest in the company, perhaps by issuing additional shares of stock. These cash flows are reported in the cash flows from financing activities portion of the cash flows statement, as shown in **TABLE 1-15**.

TABLE 1-15: THE CASH FLOWS FROM FINANCING ACTIVITIES SECTION OF A CASH FLOWS REPORT

Cash flow from financing activities	
Increase in long-term debt	$10,000
Capital stock issued	$2,000
Dividend payments	$(4,000)
Total cash flow from financing activities	$8,000
Net increase in cash	$8,630
Cash at beginning of year	$1,370
Cash at end of year	$10,000

Net Change in Cash Position

The final section of a cash flows statement is the cash reconciliation, which shows the net increase or decrease in a company's cash position added to its beginning of the year cash to reach the cash balance presented on the year-end balance sheet (see **TABLE 1-1**). As we will discuss in Chapter 7, the net change in cash has great significance to investors, bankers, and others looking to establish or maintain a financial relationship with a company.

In Conclusion

The financial statements discussed in this chapter (and in the remainder of this book) can provide you with more information than you probably thought possible, if you only know how to read them.

The next six chapters, Chapters 2 through 7, explain in detail the format, content, and analysis of each of the three financial statements discussed above. Remember that "reading" a financial statement really means analyzing a financial statement. Giving you the tools you need to effectively and efficiently "read" a financial statement is what this book is all about.

Part 2

Striking a Balance

The balance sheet balances assets to liabilities and equity. It plays a very important role in the analysis of a company and its financial performance. In the next two chapters, we discuss the balance sheet, its components, and how we can dig into its numbers to measure a company's financial success or failure.

Chapter 2

The Balance Sheet

"Honesty is the best policy—when there is money in it."

—Mark Twain

The Purpose of a Balance Sheet

A balance sheet is one of the standard financial reports prepared by all publicly traded companies and optionally by privately held businesses. It is a very valuable financial statement, presenting a fairly clear picture of the company's financial well-being on the date specified in the heading.

The primary purpose of a balance sheet is to provide information on a company's liquidity (its ability to pay its obligations in the short-run), assets (what the company owns), liabilities (what it owes), and the net worth of the business. Another major function of a balance sheet, especially for public companies, is to fulfill part of its SEC reporting requirements (see Chapter 1 for more information on SEC-required financial report elements).

A well-constructed balance sheet answers a number of questions for its stockholders, creditors, employees, and potential investors:

- Can the company fulfill its financial obligations?
- How much money has been invested in the company in the past?

- Does the company have too much debt for its cash position?
- What type of assets does the company own and how have they been financed?

How to dig into a balance sheet to answer these and other relevant balance sheet questions is covered in Chapter 3 of this book. In this chapter, we will look at what's included on the balance sheet and why.

The Philosophy of the Balance Sheet

The main concept underlying a balance sheet is based on the simple fact that any business must earn or pay for any asset it acquires. For example, when a company buys new capital assets, its assets are increased. If a company uses cash to pay for the new asset, total assets are reduced, resulting in no net change to assets. If the asset is purchased through borrowing or issuing stock, liabilities or equity (respectively) would be increased, preserving the balance of the balance sheet.

A balance sheet must, well, balance. The total of the assets must be exactly equal to the total of the accounts used to acquire those assets, which are the liabilities and the shareholders' equity. To put this into a simple formula, on a balance sheet:

Assets = Liabilities + Shareholders' equity

In other words, if a company lists $100,000 in assets, the total of its liabilities and its shareholders' equity must equal $100,000.

The Data on a Balance Sheet

I think it has been established fairly well that a balance sheet reports the balances of a company's assets and its liabilities and shareholders' equity. However, it is not enough to simply give a total of each of these areas; some detail, or what are called categories, must be reported for the balance sheet to provide any information of value. It is simply not enough to know what the totals are for these accounts and that they balance. There must also be information on the various categories within each of these areas so that some analysis can be made on how a company is managing its capital. Technically, a balance sheet that details the categories of assets, liabilities, and shareholders' equity is called a classified balance sheet.

TABLE 2-1 shows the balance sheet for Dogs on the Run, Inc. a corporation that operates hot dog carts on the sidewalks of its city. As of the end of the year, DTR held $165,000 in assets which was offset by the same amount of liabilities and owner's equity. *Note:* For companies that are not corporations (such as sole proprietorships or partnerships), the equity section of the balance sheet looks quite different.

TABLE 2-1: A SAMPLE BALANCE SHEET

Dogs on the Run, Inc.
Balance Sheet as of December 31, 2002

Assets
Current assets

Cash	$10,000
Catering accounts receivable	$2,000
Inventory	$5,000
Total current assets	$17,000

Fixed assets

Equipment	$82,000
Buildings	$73,000
(Less accumulated depreciation)	–$12,000
Total fixed assets	$143,000
Intangible assets	$5,000
Total assets	$165,000

TABLE 2-1: A SAMPLE BALANCE SHEET (CONTINUED)

Dogs on the Run, Inc.
Balance Sheet as of December 31, 2002

Liabilities and shareholders' equity

Liabilities

Current liabilities

Accounts payable	$5,000
Taxes payable	$7,000
Total current liabilities	$12,000
Long-term liabilities	
Long-term loans	$60,000
Total liabilities	$72,000
Shareholders' equity	
Common stock	$80,000
Retained earnings	$13,000
Total shareholders' equity	$93,000
Total liabilities and shareholders' equity	$165,000

Assets

Not everything a business buys is necessarily an asset. An asset is an economic resource that is held for the purpose of generating economic benefits for its owner. Money (including money owed to a business), inventory (in this case, hot dogs and buns), buildings, equipment (such as hot dog carts), and even special licenses can all be considered assets if they are used to generate revenues.

Current Assets

A current asset is any asset that is cash or can be converted into cash within a single operations cycle or one year, whichever is longer. An operations cycle is the time it takes a company to buy or produce a product, sell that product, and collect payment from a customer, which can be anywhere from two weeks to two years, depending on the business.

Creditors and potential shareholders closely watch this asset category since day-to-day operations, short-term debt, interest payments, and dividends are funded with a company's current assets. If a company falls short of cash, funds must be raised through borrowing (which could include extending its accounts payable payment cycle), aggressively collecting its accounts receivable, or seeking additional investments.

The most commonly reported current asset categories included on a balance sheet are:

CASH AND CASH EQUIVALENTS: This asset is generally understood by just about everyone. However, cash can be more than just cash money. The cash category in the current assets section of a balance statement may also include bank checking accounts, any undeposited checks received, bearer bonds, deposits in money market accounts, and just about any asset that can be readily and easily converted into cash. Certain other assets, like certificates of deposit (CDs) and securities with maturities shorter than 90 days, are also included in the cash section of the balance sheet as cash equivalents. If there are enough cash equivalents, and a company wants to make a distinction between cash and cash equivalents, cash equivalents may be listed separately on the balance sheet.

ACCOUNTS RECEIVABLE: Accounts receivable (A/R) represents the money owed to a company by its customers for goods and services delivered. For many businesses, credit sales are increasing all the time. The length of the credit may be short (up to 30 days) or long (in some industries as long as 180 days), but until payment is received, the amount owed is recorded as an account receivable. For example, whenever DTR provides catering services, an invoice is sent to the customer with payment instructions (like 15-day terms). Until the customer pays the invoice, the sales amount is classified in accounts receivable. On occasion, an A/R account may not be paid, which is why some companies list a reserve (set aside funds) against bad debts. That reserve is shown as a negative amount on the balance sheet to reduce the A/R balance and to show a truer net value for this asset, based on the company's past collections experience. Be aware that not every company has A/R balances; businesses that operate solely on a cash basis will show more in their cash balances and will not have A/R amounts at all.

SHORT-TERM INVESTMENTS: Should a company have too much cash on hand, it may be able to invest some of it in certificates of deposit (CDs), bonds, or other investments that will mature within the next 12 months. If all or part of a long-term investment will mature in the next year, that part would also be included in the current assets portion of the balance sheet.

INVENTORY: For a retail business, inventory is everything purchased for resale, but not yet sold. For manufacturing companies, the raw materials and other items that are directly used in producing its product are included in its inventory category. Whether the company is producing automobiles, steel bridges, or hot dogs, the materials that go into the finished product are carried as inventory. The inventory category also includes any work-in-progress or parts of a company's finished product that are still in work (plus any value added, such as labor, to a point in the production process). For DTR, for example, inventory is wieners, buns, wrappers, and all of the other makings that go into a finished hot dog. Investors tend to look at inventory as a current asset fairly skeptically because its liquidity is often questionable along with the fact that inventory is commonly valued at its original cost rather than its market value. In addition, as discussed later, the final inventory number that appears on the balance sheet is the result of accounting decisions; different decisions would produce a substantially different value for inventory.

PREPAID EXPENSES: On occasion a company may pay ahead expenses, receive a large credit for materials returned to a vendor, or pay a deposit for some services. In these cases, the portion of the prepayment that has not been used up remains on the balance sheet. The most common examples of prepaid expenses are rent and insurance, which are typically paid in advance.

Inventory Accounting Methods

In the accounting world, inventory can be valued using a variety of accounting methods. The primary methods used are First-In/First-Out or FIFO (pronounced as "feye-fo," oddly enough), Last-In/First-Out or LIFO (pronounced as "leye-fo," as strange as that may seem), and some form of average cost. Companies are not allowed to switch back and forth between inventory valuation methods willy-nilly, but they can change with the IRS's permission. And whichever method a company uses on its income tax filings must be the same method used on its published financial reports.

The FIFO accounting method assumes that the inventory item that was purchased or produced first (meaning at the oldest item price) is sold first. The FIFO method of inventory accounting generally tends to show a higher value of the inventory on the balance sheet, at least when prices are going up. When the oldest (and cheapest) items are considered sold first, that leaves the latest, more expensive items in inventory and in the ending balance of the inventory figure on the balance sheet. For example, under the FIFO method, if wieners recently went up from $2.00 a dozen to $2.50 a dozen, our hot dog vendor uses up its $2.00 wieners first (at least on paper) and values its wieners on hand at $2.50 per dozen.

The LIFO accounting method assumes the opposite of FIFO—that the most recently purchased or produced item is sold first. Using LIFO tends to decrease the value of the inventory on the balance sheet, because the oldest (and cheapest) items are considered to comprise the inventory. If our hot dog vendor used the LIFO method, the $2.50 per dozen wieners are used first (at least in the accounting records) and the inventory is valued at the older $2.00 per dozen price, which results in a lower ending balance of inventory on the balance sheet.

The primary reason a company may choose either LIFO or FIFO has to do with inflation. In an inflationary time, FIFO tends to better state the true approximate value of a company's ending inventory. Conversely, in an inflationary period, LIFO may not be the most reliable valuation method for inventory because it probably doesn't truly reflect the goods' current worth.

The third inventory accounting method is average cost (also called weighted average cost), which is by far the easiest to understand and apply. Average cost methods multiply each inventory item by its purchase price, total the results, and divide that dollar figure by the total number of units in inventory to determine an average inventory unit cost. For example, if our hot dog vendor has 25 dozen hot dogs in inventory at $2.00 a dozen and 15 dozen at $2.50 per dozen, its total inventory value is calculated as (2.00 × 25) + (2.50 × 15), or $87.50. The average unit cost would be computed by dividing $87.50 by 40 dozen hot dogs, or about $2.19 per dozen. The average cost method results will fall somewhere between the LIFO and FIFO values for the same inventory.

Current assets are the liquid assets of a business. Those assets that can be converted into cash, primarily through sales or maturity (like a bond or a certificate of deposit), in less than one year are considered liquid. The assets that require more than one year to convert to cash are categorized as non-liquid, or long-term, assets.

In addition to those three valuation techniques, nearly all companies use the "lower of cost or market" method to value each item in inventory. These companies write down their inventory when its replacement cost falls below the actual original purchase cost. If prices have plummeted, you can bet that the company will write down its inventory to reflect the current market price.

Long-Term Assets (Non-Current Assets)

Long-term assets are those that require more than a year to convert into cash. Long-term assets are reported separately on the balance sheet primarily to exclude them from current assets. Most long-term assets are not held for conversion to cash anyway. The assets included in this category are the capital equipment, furniture, buildings, and intangible assets that are applied by a company to produce a profit.

The assets you will find listed as long-term assets include:

FIXED ASSETS: This asset category (often referred to as "property, plant, and equipment") includes things like machinery, buildings, land, equipment, and office furniture that have useful lives of more than one year. Fixed assets are valued at their cost of acquisition, which includes all of the expenses incurred by a company to put the fixed asset in service.

ACCUMULATED DEPRECIATION: This negative amount appears on a balance sheet to reflect the reduction in value of fixed assets as their useful lives are consumed. Land is the only fixed asset that is not depreciated, since its useful life is considered infinite. While it may not sound much like an asset, depreciation is included in the long-term assets portion of the balance sheet as a contra-asset to show the remaining value of fixed assets.

INTANGIBLE OR OTHER ASSETS: This category, which is also referred to as intellectual property on some balance sheets, includes non-physical assets, rights, and licenses that the company owns or controls. A common intangible asset is goodwill, which puts a value on a company's reputation, longevity, and how well it is thought of in its industry or community. Other forms of intangible assets are patents, copyrights, and franchises. For example, let's say that DTR has negotiated an exclusive license with several companies to place hot dog carts on or in front of their premises during the lunch hour. For DTR, these licenses are a key to their success and included in their intangible assets. Intangible assets are difficult to value, primarily because they are intangible and are not readily sold. The formula used to value an intangible asset is unique to each company.

ACCUMULATED AMORTIZATION: Like accumulated depreciation, this contra-account appears on the balance sheet as a negative amount. This account reflects the reduction in value of the intangible assets over time.

Every industry has a different set of assets, but for the most part, the categories included on a balance sheet are the same regardless of the industry.

Liabilities

Any debt a company owes to any outside person or company is classified as a liability for financial reporting purposes. Liabilities can include bank loans, amounts owed to suppliers, and even wages owed to employees. Like assets, liabilities are separated into current and long-term categories.

On a balance sheet, liabilities provide information on how much debt a company is carrying. Potential investors look to the liabilities portion of a balance sheet to determine if a company is overly indebted (relative to its asset position) and in danger of perhaps going bankrupt (more on this in Chapter 3).

Current Liabilities

Current liabilities are those financial obligations that a company must pay off within the next year. Current liabilities typically include such things as accounts payable (money owed to suppliers or employees), the interest due on long-term debt, any portion or installments of long-term debt to be paid in the next year, current taxes owed, and on occasion, dividends to be paid to investors. The total of the current liabilities is of particular interest because it will be paid with current assets, which must be converted into cash to do so.

There are five primary categories of current liabilities:

ACCOUNTS PAYABLE: The amount of money a company owes to its suppliers. Although accounts payable is typically used for inventory-related invoices, monies due to partners and employees (not for salary, but for travel expenses and the like) are sometimes also included. In effect, accounts payable represents the costs of the business that haven't been paid yet.

ACCRUED EXPENSES: Not all bills a company receives are added to accounts payable. Basic operating expenses (like marketing, distribution, and utilities expenses) that are incurred but not yet paid appear on the balance sheet as accrued expenses.

INCOME TAXES PAYABLE: One of the primary accrued expense items is income taxes payable, which is the amount of taxes a company owes from a prior period that the company knows it must pay, but the due date is some time in the near future.

NOTES PAYABLE: In most cases, a short-term note is debt that has been taken from a line of credit or some form of revolving credit that must be repaid within the next year.

CURRENT PORTION OF LONG-TERM DEBT: If a portion, such as an installment payment or an interest payment, of a long-term debt is due within the next year, that portion gets reclassified as a current liability.

TABLE 2-2: THE LIABILITIES AND SHAREHOLDERS' EQUITY PORTION OF THE
DTR BALANCE SHEET

Liabilities and shareholders' equity	
Liabilities	
Current liabilities	
Accounts payable	$5,000
Taxes payable	$7,000
Total current liabilities	$12,000
Long-term liabilities	
Long-term loans	$60,000
Total liabilities	$72,000
Shareholders' equity	
Common stock	$80,000
Retained earnings	$13,000
Total shareholders' equity	$93,000
Total liabilities and shareholders' equity	$165,000

Long-Term Liabilities

Liabilities that aren't due within the next year are included in the long-term liabilities category on the balance sheet. Long-term liabilities are normally long-term loans obtained by a company. However, any installment payments to be made within the year are transferred to current liabilities.

Shareholders' Equity

As shown in **TABLE 2-2**, the shareholders' equity section of a balance sheet includes entries that show the owners' or shareholders' original investment in the company plus any profits generated by the company that were reinvested into the company (retained earnings) and not paid out to shareholders. The shareholder investment amount is generally expressed as the amount of capital stock outstanding, plus any additional paid-in-capital (the portion of the shareholders' original investment that exceeds the stated face value of the stock shares). Remember, this description of the equity section of the balance sheet applies only to corporations.

The shareholders' equity section of the DTR balance sheet (see **TABLE 2-2**) reflects its shareholders' initial investment as common stock held and the amount of prior years' earnings that were put back into the business (as an additional investment on behalf of the owners).

As a rule, publicly held corporations should have good business reasons for retaining all or a portion of their earnings and not paying out dividends to their shareholders. What constitutes a good business reason can vary, but expansion of the business, new product launches, and the like are typically cited.

The Un-Bottom Line

There really isn't one single bottom line on a balance sheet, except that the two halves of the report must net to zero. However, as we will discuss in Chapter 3, there can be a gold mine of information on a company's balance sheet, if you know how to excavate it.

Analyzing a Balance Sheet

"Half of analysis is 'anal.'"

—Marty Indik

Digging out the Information

Everyone has their own reasons for studying any company's financial statements. I may be looking to invest in the company by buying its stock; you may be deciding whether or not you want to loan the company money; and another person may be looking to acquire the company or merge with it. Whatever the reason, gleaning the information you need from the financial statements isn't an art form. Rather, there's a fairly simple, systematic approach to understanding how a company is doing by analyzing its financial statements.

This chapter focuses on the process of analyzing a balance sheet. Chapters 5 and 7 cover the analysis applied to income statements and cash flow statements, respectively.

Taking the Stairs

When one first begins to study a set of financial statements, there is a tendency to immediately do what is called an "elevator" analysis. This type of analysis places much too much significance on the "ups" and "downs" on a balance sheet, especially those that include one or more prior years of data.

43

The fact that sales are up, profits are down, and assets are unchanged doesn't necessarily mean that things are good, bad, improving, or going to hell in a handbasket. The numbers on any financial statement only supply the "whats" in an analysis, but the real importance and meaning of the numbers comes from the "whys" and "becauses." As the saying goes, "The devil is in the details."

When you take the time to understand a company, its industry, and its financials (what I call "taking the stairs"), only then can you begin to mine some real nuggets from the company's financial reports.

Pies Like Mom's, Inc.

First, let's get a balance sheet to analyze. **TABLE 3-1** shows the multi-year balance sheet of Pies Like Mom's, Inc. (PLM).

TABLE 3-1: A BALANCE SHEET

Pies Like Mom's, Inc.
Balance Sheet

	12/31/2002	12/31/2001	12/31/2000	12/31/1999
Assets				
Current assets				
Cash	$106,783	$96,105	$86,494	$77,845
Accounts receivable	$780,457	$702,411	$632,170	$568,953
Inventory	$192,655	$173,390	$156,051	$140,445
Prepaid expenses	$18,221	$17,674	$17,144	$16,630
Total current assets	$1,098,116	$989,580	$891,859	$803,873
Fixed assets				
Land, buildings, and equipment	$624,070	$620,381	$561,847	$508,989
Less accumulated depreciation	$36,872	$35,028	$33,277	$31,613
Net fixed assets	$587,198	$585,353	$528,570	$477,376
Other assets	$248,489	$228,865	$208,391	$191,352
Total assets	$1,933,803	$1,803,798	$1,628,820	$1,472,601

TABLE 3-1: A BALANCE SHEET (CONTINUED)

Pies Like Mom's, Inc.
Balance Sheet

	12/31/2002	12/31/2001	12/31/2000	12/31/1999
Liabilities				
Current liabilities				
Accounts payable, trade	$147,448	$132,703	$119,433	$107,490
Accounts payable, other	$25,225	$22,703	$20,432	$18,389
Accrued expenses	$25,816	$23,234	$20,911	$18,820
Short-term debt	$25,000	$25,000	$25,000	$25,000
Income taxes payable	$223,489	$201,140	$181,026	$162,923
Other current liabilities	—	$1,500	—	—
Total current liabilities	$446,978	$406,280	$366,802	$332,622
Long-term debt				
Notes payable	$225,000	$250,000	$275,000	$300,000
Total liabilities	$671,978	$656,280	$641,802	$632,622
Stockholders' equity				
Capital stock	$950,000	$950,000	$950,000	$950,000
Retained earnings	$311,825	$197,518	$37,018	$(110,021)
Total of stockholders' equity	$1,261,825	$1,147,518	$987,018	$839,979
Total liabilities and stockholders' equity	$1,933,803	$1,803,798	$1,628,820	$1,472,601

PLM operates as a wholesale bakery producing fresh baked fruit pies that are sold to local restaurants, retail bakeries, grocery stores, and club and public wholesale outlets. PLM's claim to fame is that they make all of their own fillings, using a "secret" (meaning proprietary) recipe handed down from the founder of the company, one Eloise Mulberry. PLM's products feature fresh apple, cherry, blueberry, and rhubarb pies.

Ms. Mulberry, who baked her first commercially sold pies in her own kitchen, founded PLM in 1914. The company has had steady, yet unspectacular growth, since it first began, expanding to its present location in 1920 and adding additional production facilities in 1938, 1951, and 1963. PLM modernized its plant in 1972 and again in 1999. Because it refuses to use food preservatives in its products, PLM limits its sales and distribution of its fresh pies to within 400 miles of Spokane, WA, its base of operations. In 2000, PLM entered a joint venture with UmGood, Inc., a foreign trading company, to flash freeze its fresh pies for shipment to Asian markets, where they are thawed and sold through UmGood's retail outlets.

Until 1995, PLM was a privately held firm. At that time, the company stock was offered to the public, with 60% of the capital stock still held by the children of Eloise Mulberry. PLM has failed to pay quarterly dividends to its stockholders only six times since going public.

Look over PLM's balance sheet and note anything you think may be noteworthy, good or bad. Were you impressed with their steady increase in cash? Are you concerned that their inventory keeps going up? Is it okay that accounts receivable continues to rise each year? Is it good that total equity also keeps rising? If you had any of these or other reactions to PLM's balance sheet, you are guilty of elevator analysis. It is common that the first review of a financial statement focuses on the ups and downs indicated from prior year numbers.

Applying Ratio Analysis

The more productive analysis tool to elevator analysis of a balance sheet is the use of ratio analysis, which creates mathematical relationships between certain elements on a financial statement. Ratio analysis of a financial statement generates information from which real judgments can be made.

You can't always interpret a single ratio on its own, but must combine or compare two or more ratios to understand a company's true financial situation. Ratios also have a way of begging further questions, which can't always be answered without digging into the company's management policies or operating rules.

In general, there are four categories of financial ratios:

- Liquidity
- Leverage
- Operating
- Return on investment (ROI)

We'll look at each financial ratio category and the ratio calculations included in it. The next few sections of this chapter cover the ratios used to measure and analyze liquidity and leverage. The ratios used to measure operating performance and return on investment are discussed in Chapter 5.

> Other groupings of financial ratios are risk, solvency, and profitability. I cover a few of the ratios in each of these groups as well in Chapters 5 and 7 and in Appendix B.

Measuring Liquidity

In business terms, liquidity measures how well a business is able to pay its debts using its current assets, those assets that are closest to cash, which of course include cash. Liquidity ratios provide a numerical indication of how current assets and current liabilities move through a business.

The most commonly used liquidity ratios are:

- Current ratio
- Working capital ratio
- Quick ratio
- Cash ratio

- Days receivables
- Days payables
- Inventory turnover

The Current Ratio

A company's current ratio is the mathematical relationship of its current assets to its current liabilities. In other words, the current ratio indicates how well a company can pay its current liabilities using its current assets. The current ratio is calculated by dividing the total current assets amount by the total current liabilities amount, using this formula:

Current assets / Current liabilities = Current ratio

For example, using the numbers on the PLM 2002 balance sheet, PLM's current ratio is calculated as:

$1,098,116 / $446,978 = 2.46

A current ratio of more than 1.0, such as PLM's 2.46, indicates that the company has sufficient current assets to cover its current liabilities. In contrast, a current ratio of less than 1.0 indicates that a company doesn't have enough current assets to cover its current liabilities—not a good sign. By rule of thumb, most analysts expect a company to have at least a 1.5 current ratio, with 2.0 being a common standard. However, remember that what is good for one company, may not be good for another; the rule of thumb is only a general guideline because the appropriate current ratio for a business generally varies by industry.

The result of a ratio calculation, like the 2.46 calculated above, is expressed in ratio form as 2.46:1 (or 2.46 to 1). The colon (":") is read as "to" and the first number in the ratio is generally compared to the number 1.0. For example, a .98:1 current ratio is read as .98 to 1 or slightly less than 1:1.

For the food and related products manufacturing industry, which includes manufacturing pies, the recommended or expected current ratio is 1.1. When compared to its industry's current ratio expectation, PLM is obviously high, but not shockingly so.

> For a look at the recommended current ratios for a variety of industries, visit the BizStats Web site at
>
> *www.bizstats.com/currentratios.htm.*

Working Capital Ratio

Certain information which is useful in analyzing a company's financial performance is not typically included directly on the balance sheet. On occasion these figures are included in the notes to the financial report, but in most cases, you'll need to do a bit of arithmetic to determine their values.

The primary value you may need to calculate is a company's working capital, which is calculated using the following formula:

> Current assets – Current liabilities = Working capital

Using the information from **TABLE 3-1**, we can calculate that PLM had $651,138 in working capital at the end of 2002.

> $1,098,116 – 446,978 = 651,138

A company should maintain a certain amount of working capital to maintain its liquidity. Often the desired working capital level is set for a business by a bank or another major lender, determined using a company's current ratio.

The working capital ratio, which is a liquidity ratio, indicates a company's working capital (current assets minus current liabilities) as a percentage of its total assets. The working capital ratio is calculated using the following formula:

> Working capital / Total assets = Working capital ratio

PLM's working capital ratio is calculated as:

$$\$651,138 / \$1,933,803 = 0.34$$

A working capital ratio that is less than zero typically indicates that a company has negative working capital, which normally is not a good thing. On the other hand, a very high working capital ratio isn't always good because it can indicate, for example, that the company's inventory is too high. Whether a working capital ratio is high or low is something that must be determined in comparison to other firms in a company's industry.

The Quick Ratio

This calculation is a variation of the current ratio that uses only the amount of current assets that can be quickly converted to cash (typically in the next 90 days) to calculate its relationship to the current liabilities. The asset balances used to calculate the quick ratio (cash and accounts receivable) are called quick assets because they are typically immediately available to apply to a company's liabilities. In effect, the use of only quick assets in this ratio calculation eliminates the use of the inventory balance. Inventory isn't always predictably convertible to cash, especially in industries with long product manufacturing times.

The quick ratio is also called the acid test because it's a put-up-or-shut-up indicator of whether a company could pay its current debts right away, if for some reason that became immediately necessary.

The quick ratio is calculated by dividing the total quick assets (cash and accounts receivable) by total current liabilities, using this formula:

Quick assets / Total current liabilities = Quick ratio

Using the numbers from **TABLE 3-1**, PLM's balance sheet, PLM's 2002 quick ratio is calculated as:

$$\$887,240 / \$446,978 = 1.98$$

A quick ratio of nearly two to one indicates that PLM has sufficient quick (liquid) assets to cover its current liabilities. A quick ratio less than 1.0 indicates that a company doesn't have enough ready assets to cover its current liabilities. PLM has about two times the cash and near-monies it needs to cover its short-term debts.

Most analysts use 1.0 as an indication of a healthy company, but this ratio varies by industry, as well. However, you should analyze the current ratio and the quick ratios together. A company may appear to be in fair shape according to its current ratio, but its quick ratio may tell you a totally different story.

The Cash Ratio

Another liquidity ratio is the cash ratio, and as you may have guessed already, it determines the relationship of a company's cash balances to its current liabilities. This ratio, although not as commonly used as the quick and current ratios, is useful in an industry that typically has accounts receivable cycles longer than 90 days.

The cash ratio is calculated using the following formula:

$$\text{Cash} / \text{Total current liabilities} = \text{Cash ratio}$$

Using information from **TABLE 3-1**, PLM's cash ratio is calculated as follows:

$$\$106,783 / \$446,978 = 0.24$$

With a cash ratio of 0.24, PLM has enough cash on hand to pay only 24% of its current liabilities immediately. In a tight economy, you may not want to extend long credit terms to this company. However, at the risk of repeating myself, the expected cash ratio varies by industry.

Current, Quick, and Cash Ratio Lessons

So, what have we learned about liquidity ratios? If nothing else, you now know how to determine whether or not a company is able to meet its current obligations with its current assets. Liquidity ratios above 1.0 indicate, in every case, that a company has at least enough current assets to pay off its current liabilities in the event of a financial emergency.

Days Receivable Ratio

The days receivable ratio, which is also called the receivables turn ratio, indicates how fast or slow a company's customers pay their bills. Unlike the previous ratios, a smaller number for this ratio is a good thing.

Considering that on average most companies extend 30-day payment terms to their customers, if a company has a days receivable ratio less than 30, then we can apply greater credence to its current ratio since the company is converting its receivables into cash fairly quickly. However, if the days receivable ratio is greater than 30, say 100 days, then obviously we should look harder at the company's cash ratio.

On the balance sheets published by companies that have sales, which should be virtually every company, you should find an accounts receivable balance. The accounts receivable amount shown on a balance sheet represents the amount of money owed to the company by its customers on the last day of the reporting period. If the balance sheet is a year-end report, the accounts receivable balance represents only a portion (hopefully, a small portion) of the company's total sales for the year.

Of course, depending on the company's industry, products, and any cyclical or seasonal impacts on the business, the percentage that the accounts receivable balance represents of the company's total sales will vary greatly. For example, the hot dog cart business we looked at in Chapter 2 generates mostly cash sales, but they do have an occasional catering job that can show up in accounts receivable on the balance sheet. If we assume that this business does almost 80% of its total sales volume in the summer months, we would expect accounts receivable to be relatively small (if not zero) on a December 31st statement—assuming that there weren't too many hot dog Christmas parties.

On the other hand, PLM's sales are essentially year-round, with a slight increase in sales in the winter and holiday months. Looking at PLM's balance sheet, we see that it had $780,457 in accounts receivable at the end of 2002. Jumping to conclusions, we can guess that PLM either had very good sales in the last month or so of the year, or it is having trouble collecting from its customers. But, how bad or good is this number really? Let's see.

Calculating the A/R Turns

The first step in analyzing PLM's accounts receivable balance is to calculate the number of times per year the current balance would have been completely paid off. To do that, we first need to calculate the average accounts receivable balance. The average is calculated by adding the A/R balance at the beginning of the year to that at the end of the year, and dividing by two. Using numbers from PLM's multi-year balance sheet, we determine that the average accounts receivable balance is $741,434, as shown in this example.

(Beginning A/R balance + Ending A/R balance) / 2
($780,457 + 702,411) / 2 = $741,434

So, using PLM's average accounts receivable balance of $741,434, we can calculate a ratio that indicates how many times the accounts receivable balance cycles during the year. This ratio is called the accounts receivable turn and is calculated using the following formula:

Sales / Average accounts receivable balance = Receivable turn

From PLM's income statement (see Chapter 4), we know that its gross combined sales (revenues) for the year were $1,803,270. If we divide this number by $741,434 (PLM's average A/R balance), we get the value 2.43, which indicates that PLM was able to turn over its accounts receivable balance a little more than twice during the year, per the results of this calculation:

$$\$1,803,270 / \$741,434 = 2.43$$

A receivable turn ratio of 12.0 would indicate that a company is able to collect its average accounts receivable balance approximately monthly; and a ratio of 4.0 indicates accounts receivables are cleared about once every quarter. Depending on the seasonality of the business and what the normal credit terms are in the industry, an accounts receivable turn of 2.43 may or may not be good.

Days Receivable Ratio

To convert this to a ratio that tells us about how many days worth of accounts receivable PLM is carrying, we divide the number of days in the period by the accounts receivable turn ratio using the following formula.

Accounting folks like to simplify their calculations by reducing the year to a simple structure of 30 days in each month and 12 months in a year, which yields an accounting year of 360 days. The 360-day year is used in virtually all financial ratio calculations.

Days in period / Accounts receivable turn = Days receivable

Using PLM's information, the days receivable ratio for the year is calculated as:

$$360 / 2.43 = 148.15$$

The resulting value of 148.15 indicates that PLM has approximately 148 days of uncollected accounts receivable on account at the end of the period. If our assumption is correct that the average accounts receivable balance is representative of the entire year, then we can project that PLM is currently averaging just over five months between invoicing the customer and receiving payment. It also means that for analysis purposes, we can assume that PLM will require about 150 days to convert its accounts receivable balance into cash. This means that we may not want to include accounts receivable when calculating the current and quick ratios to evaluate PLM's liquidity.

How good or bad a days receivable ratio of 148 is depends both on the seasonality of the business and on PLM's credit terms and aggressiveness in pursuing late payments. If PLM offers net 120 credit terms, which means they require the customer to pay PLM's invoices within 120 days of the invoice date, a days receivable ratio of 148 is just a bit on the long side. On the other hand, this days receivable ratio may indicate that PLM is having trouble collecting on its invoices. Typically, a days receivable ratio of 90 or more indicates that the accounts receivable balance should not be included in the current or quick asset position considerations and the cash ratio should be relied upon more.

The Days Payables Ratio

So, now we know how to test a company's performance in getting paid by its customers, but how is the company doing in paying its own bills? The days payables ratio is used to judge how on average a business meets its obligations to its trade vendors. Companies exist to produce and sell products and services, hopefully at a profit. Financial statements that indicate that a company is not paying its production suppliers regularly may also indicate a cash flow problem or, worse, a management problem.

In the same way that we used the total sales from the reporting period to calculate the accounts receivable-based ratios, to calculate the days payables ratio we use the cost of goods sold amount from the reporting period to represent the volume of direct product expenditures for the period. Applying the same logic as used in the accounts receivable turns and the days receivable ratios, we use the cost of goods sold amount from the income statement (see Chapter 4) as the total amount of product-related expenditures over the period.

The reason accounts payable, trade is used in computing this ratio is that it typically represents the bulk of payments flowing out of a company. Other payable amounts often represent less than 10% of total accounts payable.

Payable Turn

The process to calculate the days payables ratio is almost exactly that used in calculating the days receivable ratio. We calculate the payable turn ratio to determine how many times during the period a company was able to theoretically pay off its accounts payable balance completely. The payable turn ratio is calculated using this formula:

Cost of goods sold / Average accounts payable, trade =
Payable turn

First we calculate the average accounts payable, trade balance.

($147,448 + 132,703) / 2 = $140,076

PLM's cost of goods sold on its year-end income statement is $1,355,139. Dividing that figure by the average accounts payable amount yields a payables turn of 9.67. This is calculated as follows:

$1,355,139 / $140,076 = 9.67

A payable turn ratio of 9.67 indicates that PLM turned over its trade accounts payables more than nine times during the year, or the equivalent of about every 37 days. However, a more meaningful indicator of how well PLM is conserving its cash and letting it work for them, instead of the vendors, is the days payable ratio.

Days Payable Ratio

Assuming that the average accounts payable, trade amount we calculated represents a true average of the accounts payable for production materials over the reporting period, we can calculate a days payable ratio, or the number of days a company is holding a vendor's invoice before paying it. Days payable is calculated using the following formula:

Days in period / Payables turn = Days payable

Using the numbers from PLM's year-end financial reports, we can calculate its days payable ratio as follows:

360 / 9.67 = 37.23

A days payable ratio of 37.23 can suggest that PLM uses the full-length of its credit terms from vendors and suppliers. If the standard trade credit terms are 30 days in its industry, then PLM is just slightly slower in paying its production material bills. However, if credit terms have been negotiated to more than 30 days as a trade-off for ordering more production materials, say to 45 days, we can conclude that on average PLM is performing to its agreements. If the days payable ratio indicates slow payment, say a ratio around 60, the ability of the company to continue to get trade materials on credit may be at risk.

Inventory Turnover

For manufacturing and retail firms, inventory is usually the largest current asset. Inventory is typically a very costly asset—and I'm not just talking about the item costs. To have inventory on hand requires personnel and space, at the very least. A business needs people to shelve, arrange, and maintain inventory as well as a warehouse or other storage space for the inventory "in the back."

Having too much inventory around will cost more in wages and rents, but having too little inventory on hand will cost lost sales and, eventually, lost customers. So it's very important for a company to strike the right balance of inventory, holding not more than they can reasonably sell but not so little that they'll have shortfalls, backorders, and irate customers.

To measure the relative size of a corporation's inventory, we calculate their inventory turnover by dividing their cost of goods sold (from the income statement) by their average inventory. To compute average inventory, we add the beginning of the year inventory (last year's balance sheet figure) to the ending inventory (shown on the current balance sheet) and divide the result by two.

(Beginning inventory + Ending inventory) / 2 = Average inventory

Using the numbers from PLM's multi-year balance sheet, we can calculate its average inventory as follows:

($173,390 + $192,655) / 2 = $183,023

Now that we have PLM's average inventory calculated, we can figure out their inventory turnover for 2002. Using the cost of goods sold figure from their 2002 income statement, $1,355,139 (see Chapter 4), we can determine PLM's inventory turnover as shown here:

Cost of goods sold / Average inventory = Inventory turnover
$1,355,139 / $183,023 = 7.40

An inventory turnover of 7.40 means that the entire inventory is sold and repurchased a little over seven times per year. As with all the other ratios we've looked at, this number should be compared to the industry average to see if it's high, low, or just right.

Analyzing Debt

The amount of debt a business carries may or may not be a problem. While most companies are prudent in the amount of debt they have, when analyzing a company's balance sheet, the effect of any debt needs to be looked into.

Debt to Assets Ratio

The debt to assets (D/A) ratio is used to determine what percentage of a business's assets has been funded through debt as opposed to the percentage that have been funded by owners' equity. The D/A ratio is calculated using the following formula:

Total liabilities / Total assets = Debt to assets ratio

Using PLM's information from **TABLE 3-1**, PLM has $671,978 of total liabilities against $1,933,803 in total assets, which results in a D/A ratio of 0.35. This is calculated as follows:

$671,978 / 1,933,803 = 0.35

For most industries, a debt to asset ratio of 50% (0.50) or less is considered good. A higher D/A ratio may indicate an over-leveraged (too much debt for its current assets) company that may have problems in the future making its debt payments.

Debt to Equity Ratio

Perhaps a better measure than the debt to assets ratio on how leveraged a company may be is the debt to equity (D/E) ratio, which is also called the Leverage ratio. The D/E ratio measures the amount of debt a company is carrying as a percentage of its shareholders' equity. The D/E ratio is calculated using the following formula:

Total liabilities / Shareholders' equity = Debt to equity ratio

As an example, PLM (see **TABLE 3-1**) has reported that at the end of its 2002 fiscal year, it had $671,978 in total liabilities and

$1,261,825 in shareholders' equity, which computes to a D/E ratio of 0.53 as shown in the following example.

$$\$671,978 / 1,261,825 = 0.53$$

The 2002 industry average for bakery products is 2.0 (but this can vary by industry), so PLM is definitely not as leveraged as many businesses in its industry in terms of the amount of liabilities it carries against its shareholders' equity.

For a list of debt to equity and debt to asset ratios for a wide variety of industries, visit BizStats' Web site at
www.bizstats.com/corpdecurrent.htm.

Part 3

Looking at Income

The income statement can tell you much more than if the company made money or not. All you need to know is what to look for. The income statement and how it can be analyzed are discussed in Chapters 4 and 5, respectively.

Chapter 4

The Income Statement

"My problem lies in reconciling my gross
habits with my net income."

—Errol Flynn

Balancing Income to Expenses

While the balance sheet shows how well a company is able to meet its obligations (see Chapters 2 and 3), the income statement shows how well a company has performed (at least for the reported period) in carrying out its reason to be. Every company has the primary objective to produce a product or supply a service and sell it to customers at a price that should yield a profit.

The income statement measures a company's ability to produce a profit through their sales, manufacturing, and cost control activities, all of which should lead to a profit. The success or failure in any or all of these three areas has a direct impact on whether or not a company makes a profit or loses money. However, one must avoid assumptions and knee-jerk reactions to the numbers on the income statement. Sometimes what appears to be a drop in the sales volume or an increase in the cost of production or expenses may have an explanation. Digging into the numbers may yield the information that a down condition was expected and something for which the company had planned. As with all financial statements,

63

much of the information that can be determined from an income statement depends on the industry, the economy, and the market.

This chapter focuses on the contents of an income statement. Chapter 5 covers the analysis process applied to an income statement.

Pies Like Mom's, Inc.

In Chapter 3, we looked at the balance sheet for Pies Like Mom's, Inc. (PLM) and got to know a bit about it and its operations. PLM operates as a wholesale bakery producing fresh baked fruit pies that are sold to local restaurants, retail bakeries, grocery stores, and club and public wholesale outlets. PLM's claim to fame is that they make all of their own fillings, using a "secret," meaning proprietary, recipe handed down from the founder of the company, one Eloise Mulberry. PLM's products feature fresh apple, cherry, blueberry, and rhubarb pies.

TABLE 4-1 shows PLM's latest income statement. Look over PLM's income statement and mark or jot down anything you think may be noteworthy, good or bad. What did you see? Are you impressed with their steady growth in sales and net income? Are you concerned that food costs keep rising? How about the steady increase in non-direct expenses? Do you think there is a problem?

If you had any of the above reactions to PLM's income statement, remember that elevator analysis generally won't give you answers, only questions. Would you feel better about the numbers had PLM not included prior years?

The Income Statement

TABLE 4-1: AN INCOME STATEMENT

Pies Like Mom's, Inc.
Income Statement for the Year Ended

	12/31/2002	12/31/2001	12/31/2000	12/31/1999
Revenues				
Wholesale sales	$1,707,095	$1,501,498	$1,295,196	$1,132,252
Retail sales	$96,175	$84,790	$73,446	$62,143
Gross revenues	$1,803,270	$1,586,288	$1,368,642	$1,194,395
Cost of sales				
Food costs	$1,315,250	$1,246,175	$1,233,713	$1,221,376
Other direct costs	$39,889	$35,989	$32,476	$29,312
Total cost of sales	$1,355,139	$1,282,164	$1,266,189	$1,250,688
Gross profit	$448,131	$304,124	$102,453	$(56,293)
Operating expenses				
Selling and administrative expenses	$7,978	$7,198	$6,495	$5,862
Depreciation	$36,872	$35,028	$33,185	$29,866
Total operating expenses	$44,850	$42,226	$39,680	$35,728
Operating income	$403,281	$261,898	$62,773	$(92,021)
Interest expense	$13,500	$15,000	$16,500	$18,000
Income before taxes	$389,781	$246,898	$46,273	$(110,021)
Income taxes	$77,956	$49,380	$9,255	$0
Net income	$311,825	$197,518	$37,018	$(110,021)

Examining the Data

Let's take a closer look at the account categories included on the income statement in **TABLE 4-1**.

Revenues

The value of the sales revenue comes from the prices charged to customers for the goods or services sold during the reported period. Sales are booked or recorded when the sale to the customer is made and not when the customer pays, necessarily. In a retail operation, of course, these two parts of the sale occur almost simultaneously. However, in a wholesale operation or a manufacturing business, writing up the order, recording the sale, producing the good or delivering the service, shipping the good, billing the customer, and processing the customer's payment typically occur at different times separated by days, weeks, or months.

When a credit sale is recorded, the amount to be owed by the customer begins its life as an accounts receivable entry. Of course, the customer really doesn't owe anything until the good or service is shipped or received. The accounts receivable amount included on the balance sheet (see Chapter 2) reflects those goods or services that have been shipped or delivered and payment has not been received yet.

In PLM's income statement (see **TABLE 4-1**), sales have been separated into wholesale, PLM's primary business, and retail so that these two activities can be tracked individually. Some companies get even more creative and detail the sales, discounts, returns, and other sales-related amounts on their income statements. This is done either to highlight significant activities or for tracking purposes, like PLM's sales.

In a simpler income statement, like that in **TABLE 4-2**, revenue from sales is commonly listed as a single line item.

TABLE 4-2: AN INCOME STATEMENT
FOR A SMALL BUSINESS

Small Biz, Inc.
Income Statement: For the Year Ended December 31, 2002

Sales	$115,000
Cost of sales	$35,000
Gross profit	$80,000
Operating expense	$27,000
Depreciation expense	$3,000
Operating income	$50,000
Interest expense	$1,000
Income taxes	$4,000
Net income	$45,000

Cost of Sales

You will also see the cost of sales category listed as cost of goods sold, which fairly summarizes what this category represents. Cost of sales includes the costs that are incurred to produce or purchase the goods or services a company sold (and included in its sales category).

The value assigned to cost of sales is directly tied to the inventory valuation method used by the company, such as FIFO, LIFO, or average cost (see Chapter 2 for a complete discussion of these inventory valuation methods). For example, under the FIFO method (first in/first out), cost of sales would reflect mainly the "first-in" costs, since those are the first out. This typically results in a lower cost of sales than would be reported using the other valuation methods. Conversely, the LIFO valuation method (last in/first out) usually results in the highest cost of sales, as the "last-in" items are the first to go (since generally we live in a world with inflation, the latest purchases are typically the most expensive). And valuing cost of sales using an average cost method would produce results somewhere in between those of FIFO and LIFO. As you can see, the accounting method chosen to value inventory has a direct impact on the value of cost of sales, and a corresponding direct impact on a company's net income.

Cost of sales may also reflect any valuation adjustments made to a company's inventory. If a company disposes of a part of its inventory or adjusts its value downward, the value of the disposed inventory or the difference between the old and new valuation is a cost of production and is reported in cost of sales. For example, if a manufacturer decides to cease production of one of its older products, the company no longer needs any leftover parts, assemblies, and raw materials used solely on that product. The company can attempt to resell this portion of the inventory, but in almost every case, they can expect to get only pennies on the dollar, if anything at all. The difference between the cost of the obsolete inventory and what the company is able to get for it, by selling, recycling, or scrapping it, is added to the cost of sales amount for that period or in some cases listed in a one-time charge section of the income statement.

Retail operators may also include what is called shrinkage in the cost of sales amount. Shrinkage is a generic term for the quantity and value of items that are stolen, damaged, obsolete, or outdated. Depending on the severity of its shrinkage problem, a company might record its shrinkage as an operating expense.

Remember that inventory is a primary entry on the balance sheet, but only its period-ending value is reported there. So, any inventory write-downs need to be recorded as a cost (either cost of sales or as an expense) to offset the income generated for the period in which the adjustment occurred.

Gross Profit

Gross profit is the net of the sales and the cost of sales for a period. This number is important because it is a first indication of whether a company is selling enough of its products or services to cover its production costs. Gross profit is calculated as follows:

Sales – Cost of sales = Gross profit

A positive gross profit reflects that a company is probably pricing its products correctly and is able to sell them at a sufficient rate to cover its costs. However, a negative gross profit amount should be a red flag that something is wrong, especially if the inventory value is rising (see Chapters 2 and 3).

A negative gross profit indicates a variety of other problems, the least of which may be that the economy has shifted and demand for the company's goods or services decreased faster than the company was able to react to the change. Another problem may be the product pricing (too high—or in a weird case, too low), production scheduling or management issues, or one or more of the company's products is or is becoming obsolete.

Operating Expenses

Any selling, general, or administrative expense incurred by a company that is not interest, taxes on income, or directly related to the production of a good or service is included in the operating expenses or other expenses category. Technically, depreciation is also an operating expense, but often that amount is reported separately.

The types of expenses included in the operating expenses amount are non-production wages, legal fees, office rent, the share of the utilities not used in production, pens, paper clips, and the like. In effect, operating expenses represent a company's overhead amount.

Depreciation Expense

What differentiates depreciation expense from other operating expenses is that depreciation is a non-cash expense. Where other types of expenses reduce a company's cash balance, depreciation reduces the net value of the company's buildings, machinery, equipment, tools, desks, chairs, computers, automobiles, trucks, and other fixed assets (those assets with a service life longer than three years typically). In essence, depreciation is the "cost" of using these assets during the reported period.

Depreciation Methods

Depreciation is an accounting method used to allocate the cost of owning an asset over its useful life. If a company buys a large piece of manufacturing equipment that has a useful life of 15 years, it knows two things about this item: 1) that the item will possibly need to be replaced in 15 years; and 2) that after each year of its life, this item is not worth what was originally paid for it. Depreciation addresses both of these issues, but in terms of the financial statements, it addresses the latter more directly. In effect, depreciation measures the loss in value of an asset over its useful lifetime.

Just about any asset with a useful life longer than three years can be depreciated, subject to the IRS and GAAP guidelines. Depreciable assets include things like office furniture and equipment, buildings, machinery, computers, cars, trucks, and the like. Perhaps the largest exception to this is land. Land cannot be depreciated because conventional wisdom states that land doesn't become obsolete, wear out, or diminish in value, in most cases.

There are a variety of methods used to depreciate an asset. Perhaps the most common, and certainly easiest to apply, is straight-line depreciation. This method simply takes the initial cost of an item (including all costs of acquisition—freight, sales taxes, installation charges, etc.) and divides it by the number of years in its useful life. For example, if a company purchases an automated machining tool for its manufacturing area for $600,000 that has an estimated useful life of 10 years, the straight-line depreciation for this item would be $60,000 per year for the next 10 years, or until the machinery becomes obsolete or unusable. If after its useful life, the machinery has a value to a salvage dealer or another company and can be sold for its salvage value, this reduces the depreciable amount of its final year. If the machinery is totally without value, it is written off completely.

Some companies prefer to use an accelerated depreciation method so that assets can be depreciated more quickly than using the straight-line method. An accelerated depreciation method provides a greater amount of depreciation in the early years of an asset's life and, as the asset ages, smaller amounts in its later years. The two general types of accelerated depreciation are the declining-balance and sum-of-the-years digits methods.

DECLINING-BALANCE DEPRECIATION METHOD: This accelerated depreciation method multiplies the asset's net book value (asset cost minus all prior depreciation) by a constant depreciation rate over the estimated life of the asset.

SUM-OF-THE-YEARS DIGITS DEPRECIATION METHOD: This accelerated depreciation method writes off the entire asset cost, adjusted for any possible salvage value, using a varying percentage rate over the asset's life.

For tax purposes, a lot of companies use the accelerated depreciation tables published by the IRS, a method called MACRS (pronounced "makers," and meaning modified accelerated cost recovery system). This method groups assets into categories based on their useful lives; all assets in a single category follow the same accelerated depreciation schedule, similar to the sum-of-the-years digits method.

TABLE 4-3 shows a comparison of the straight-line and the declining-balance depreciation methods for the first five years of our $600,000 manufacturing machinery. The declining-balance depreciation method reduces the book value of an asset at a faster rate in the item's early years of service—much in the same way that a new car depreciates dramatically the minute you drive it off the car lot.

TABLE 4-3: STRAIGHT-LINE DEPRECIATION VERSUS DECLINING-BALANCE DEPRECIATION

	STRAIGHT-LINE DEPRECIATION		DECLINING-BALANCE DEPRECIATION	
Year	Depreciation	Y/E Book Value	Depreciation	Y/E Book Value
1	$60,000	$540,000	$120,000	$480,000
2	$60,000	$480,000	$96,000	$384,000
3	$60,000	$420,000	$76,800	$307,200
4	$60,000	$360,000	$61,440	$245,760
5	$60,000	$300,000	$49,152	$196,608

The sum-of-the-years digits accelerated depreciation method creates a fraction using a sum of the digits for each depreciable year as its denominator and the depreciable year as its numerator. (It's not as complicated as it sounds.)

If an asset has a 10-year service life, the sum of the years digits is calculated as follows:

$$10 + 9 + 8 + 7 + 6 + 5 + 4 + 3 + 2 + 1 = 55$$

So the denominator of our depreciation factor for the life of a 10-year asset is 55. Each year's depreciation is then calculated by using the number of the depreciable year (counting down from the total number of years). The factor used for the first year would be 10/55 (or about 18.2%); the second year would be 9/55 (or about 16.4%); the third year would be 8/55 (or about 14.5%); and so on down to 55 (or a bit less than 2%). **TABLE 4-4** shows a comparison of the straight-line depreciation method and the sum-of-the-years digits depreciation method.

TABLE 4-4: STRAIGHT-LINE DEPRECIATION VERSUS
SUM-OF-THE-YEARS DIGITS DEPRECIATION

Year	Straight-Line Depreciation			Sum-of-the-Years Digits Depreciation		
	Rate	Depreciation	Y/E Book Value	Rate	Depreciation	Y/E Book Value
1	10%	$60,000	$540,000	18.18% (10/55)	$109,080	$490,920
2	10%	$60,000	$480,000	16.36% (9/55)	$98,160	$392,760
3	10%	$60,000	$420,000	14.55% (8/55)	$87,300	$305,460
4	10%	$60,000	$360,000	12.73% (7/55)	$76,380	$229,080
5	10%	$60,000	$300,000	10.91% (6/55)	$65,460	$163,620

Notice how in **TABLE 4-4**, the sum-of-the-years digits depreciation method depreciates nearly 50% of the assets value in just the
first three years. Comparing that to the straight-line method, notice
how the sum-of-the-years digits depreciation method results in a
lower book value for the asset in the third year and beyond, which is
why the sum-of-the-years digits method is called an accelerated
depreciation method.

Operating Income

This is one of the more important numbers on the income statement. A company's operating income is an indication of its earning
power from its product or service operations. Operating income is
calculated as follows:

Gross profit – (Operating expense + Depreciation) =
Operating income

Operating income measures a company's ability to produce
profits from the operations it was formed to carry out, whether they
be producing products or delivering services. It is calculated without
interest and tax expenses to focus this subtotal on the income earned
from operations only and not other profit sources, such as investments and other non-production-related areas.

Operating income is also referred to as operating profit or earnings before interest and taxes (EBIT).

Interest Expense

This category is fairly self-explanatory. Interest expense includes
the interest paid on loans, notes, bonds, and so forth, which are the
short- and long-term liabilities listed on the balance sheet. This category may also include loan fees, such as loan origination fees and
loan points charged by the lender.

Income Tax Expense

Any income taxes paid to federal, state, or local taxing authorities during the reported period are included in the income tax expense category. Other types of taxes, such as sales tax paid, property taxes, or disability, unemployment, or Social Security taxes paid as part of employee payroll, are included in the operating expense entry.

Net Income

Net income, which is also called net profit, net earnings, or the bottom line, reflects the profits generated by a company after its interest and income tax expenses are deducted from its operational income. Net income is calculated as follows:

Operating income – (Interest + Income tax) = Net income

A positive net income indicates the company made a net profit from its overall operations. On the other hand, a negative net income, which is never a good thing, shows that the company wasn't able to generate enough income to cover all of its expenses. Chapter 5 looks at the ways both a positive and negative net income can be interpreted.

Net income is not the same as cash (contrary to popular belief), largely because of the accrual nature of financial statements. Whatever the net income amount, it is linked to the balance sheet (see Chapter 2), where it is shown as either distributions to shareholders or added to retained earnings, and the cash flows statement (see Chapter 6), where its impact on a company's cash position is calculated.

Break-Even Analysis

Although not necessarily an analytical tool used by analysts to study a company's financial statements, the break-even analysis is a very useful tool for business owners to use when studying their own financials.

The break-even point for any business is where total costs (TC) equal total revenues (TR), or at least that's what the economists tell us. In business terms, the break-even point is where a company's sales volume is high enough and generating enough revenue to operate the business without a loss. At the break-even point, a business isn't making any profits, but then it isn't losing money either.

If a company is at the break-even point, producing and selling (the key word here is selling) more product units should produce a profit and selling fewer units than the break-even quantity produces a loss.

The following are the operating elements that go into the break-even analysis:

SELLING PRICE (SP): The price at which each good or service is sold. SP, which is expressed as dollars per unit, is used to determine total revenue (TR) and gross profit or contribution margin (CM) per unit.

VARIABLE COSTS (VC): Variable costs include direct material, labor costs, manufacturing overhead, transportation, and selling costs per unit. VC is expressed as dollars per unit.

FIXED COSTS (FC): Costs that remain constant for a given period of time and a certain production level. FC includes general and administrative costs, interest, and depreciation. FC is expressed as a dollar lump sum.

UNITS (X): The number of units produced and sold. Break-even analysis assumes that all units produced are sold.

AVERAGE FIXED COSTS (AFC): The prorated share of fixed costs over a given number of units in a period. AFC is expressed as dollars per unit.

AVERAGE TOTAL COST (ATC): The sum of unit VC and AFC, which represents the total allocated costs per unit. ATC is expressed as dollars per unit.

TOTAL COST (TC): The sum of all variable costs and fixed costs incurred to produce a number of units in a given period.

CONTRIBUTION MARGIN (CM): The amount of the selling price remaining after unit variable cost is removed. In other words, SP – VC = CM. CM is expressed either as dollars per unit or as a percentage (using the equation CM / SP).

TOTAL REVENUE (TR): The quantity sold times the selling price.

To calculate a break-even point for a company, follow these steps:

1. Calculate the break-even quantity (the quantity needed to cover fixed costs):

B/E X = FC / (SP – VC) or X = FC / CM

2. Calculate the break-even total revenue in dollars:

TR = X × SP

So let's assume that BreakEven Corporation, which sells boxes, has $100,000 in fixed costs. Each box sells for $5.00, and the variable cost associated with each box is $3.00.

The break-even quantity for the company would equal 50,000 units, as shown in the following example.

$100,000 / ($5.00 – $3.00) = 50,000

The break-even total revenue in dollars for BreakEven Corporation is $250,000.

50,000 × $5.00 = $250,000

Chapter 5

Analyzing Income Statements

*"The ability to make good decisions is gained from
the experience of making bad decisions."*

—Ron Price

Ratio Analysis and the Income Statement

As discussed in Chapter 4, the income statement reports a company's ability to generate income and yield profits over a given period. The ability to generate earnings is a fundamental part of what every business is about and a key component in a company's overall worth. Because of this, you should understand the relationships of the numbers on the income statement and how they tie back to the balance sheet and other financial statements in a company's annual report.

The ratios used to analyze an income statement are not all that different than those used to analyze a balance sheet (see Chapter 3) in that they create ratios between income statement amounts or between an income statement amount and one from the balance sheet. When analyzing an income statement, the focus is on a company's profitability (the operating ratios) and efficiency (the return on investment ratios).

The ratios and tools used to analyze an income statement measure a variety of a company's operations during the reported period (which is typically one year). In the following sections, we look at the ratios used to measure efficiency, profitability, and also solvency.

Times Interest Earned Ratio

The times interest earned (TIE) ratio, which is also called the interest coverage ratio, indicates the relationship between a company's earnings before interest and taxes (EBIT—see Chapter 4) and the amount of interest the company paid to outside creditors, lenders, and bondholders. It is used as an indication of a company's solvency.

The TIE ratio is calculated as follows:

EBIT / Interest payments = Times interest earned ratio

The TIE ratio tells current and future lenders and bondholders how well a company's earnings cover their interest payments. If a company has a relatively low TIE ratio, say 1:1, then it takes all of a company's earnings just to pay its interest obligations, which is not good news to current and future lenders and bondholders. On the other hand, a TIE ratio of 13:1 states that a company is able to generate 13 times more earnings than it has to pay out as interest amounts.

Using the number from the income statement of Pies Like Mom's, Inc. (PLM) from Chapter 4, we find that PLM had $13,500 of interest expense generated from the interest on its long-term debt and an EBIT (operating income) of $403,281. Its TIE ratio is calculated as:

403,281 / 13,500 = 29.9

In other words, PLM's times interest earned ratio is 29.9 to 1 or 29.9:1. This indicates that PLM is generating way higher earnings than it owes in interest and should have no problem meeting its interest expense obligations, all things being equal.

Investors also use the TIE ratio as an indication of whether a company may soon go bankrupt or not. A company's inability to pay its interest payments, which usually means pay its long-term debt obligations, is a sure-fire indication that the company may need to seek protection from its creditors under bankruptcy laws

Economists and management accountants have a phrase they like to use: *ceteris paribus*, which is a Latin phrase meaning "all other things being equal." This phrase is commonly used to freeze out all other factors that could possibly change and impact the outcome of the current calculation.

Profitability Ratios

The primary purpose of the income statement is to report a company's profits or losses. However, just knowing that a company made a profit or suffered a loss may not tell the whole story. It is easier to understand a company's profitability when it's expressed as a percentage (ratio). A percentage, especially a percentage rate of change, allows you to compare one year's performance to performance in other years. A ratio provides a basis of comparison for comparing one company to another as well.

To really understand a company's profitability, a variety of ratios, called profit margins, are used. The three most common profit margins are:

- Gross margin
- Operating margin
- Net margin

Gross Margin
The gross margin profitability ratio can be used to analyze a company's efficiency in producing and distributing its products or

Financial Statements for Non-Financial People

services. Gross margin is calculated as gross profit (revenues minus costs) divided by revenue, using the following formula:

Gross profit / Total net revenues = Gross margin

Since gross margin effectively measures the percentage of revenue that remains after production costs are removed, it is a good indicator of how effectively a company is managing its production and distribution costs.

Using the revenue and sales numbers from Mike's Bikes income statement (see **TABLE 5-1**), we see that Mike's Bikes had gross revenues in 2002 of $520,700 and gross profit of $381,660. Therefore, Mike's 2002 gross margin is calculated as:

381,660 / 520,700 = .733 or 73.3%

A gross margin of 73.3% indicates that Mike's Bikes costs of sales represent only 26.7% of its net sales, which seems very good. However, at the risk of repeating myself, this result would have to be compared to other companies in the same industry or those also selling bikes. A 2001 issue of *Bicycle Retailer* magazine reported that the industry average gross margin for bicycle retailers was 34.4%. Given this number, it seems that Mike's Bikes is doing very well indeed at over twice the industry average.

TABLE 5-1: 2002 INCOME STATEMENT
FROM MIKE'S BIKES

Mike's Bikes Income Statement for the Year Ended 12/31/2002

Revenues

Retail sales	$474,525
Service sales	$46,175
Total revenues	$520,700

Cost of sales

Retail operations	$79,240
Service operations	$59,800
Total cost of sales	$139,040
Gross profit	$381,660

Operating expenses

Selling and administrative expenses	$15,250
Depreciation	$5,245
Total operating expenses	$20,495
Operating income	$361,165
Interest expense	$4,095
Income before taxes	$357,070
Income taxes	$83,965
Net income	$273,105

Operating Margin

A company's operating margin ratio indicates the quality of its operations, in terms of its fixed costs (such as its facilities and other long-term production or sales-related assets), its gross margin, or both. In order to have a high operating margin, a business either must be operating with relatively low fixed costs or a relatively high gross margin, especially when compared with other firms in its industry. Companies that report an operating margin relatively higher than their competitors are deemed to be more productive or sales-efficient and should typically have an advantage over their competitors.

The operating margin ratio is calculated by dividing operating income by gross profit, using the following formula:

Operating income / Total net revenues = Operating margin

Using Mike's Bikes information from **TABLE 5-1**, we can calculate its operating margin as follows:

361,165 / 520,700 = .694 or 69.4%

The bicycle retailers trade association indicates that the operating margin ranges from .30 to .40 (30% to 40%) amongst most highly successful companies. In comparison, Mike's Bikes, with an operating margin of 69.4%, is doing incredibly well in terms of its operating margin.

Net Margin

The last of the profitability ratios is net margin. As you might assume from its name, this ratio measures the overall profitability of a business using the bottom line. Once again, this number by itself is not really all that meaningful. To place any relative value on a company's net margin, you must compare it to the average net margin of the company's industry.

The net margin ratio is calculated using the following formula:

Net income / Total net revenues = Net margin

The net margin ratio shows net income (bottom-line profit) as a percentage of total net revenues. For Mike's Bikes, the net margin calculation is:

273,105 / 520,700 = .524 or 52.4%

The higher a company's net margin ratio is (compared to its

industry average), the more competitive the company is in the market place. Net margin is also a good ratio for comparing a company's profitability performance year-to-year. Net margin for a single year may indicate something good or bad about a company, but when compared to previous years, you can determine if the company has an improving profitability trend or not. One good net margin year could be the result of many things, but a strong net margin that continues year-to-year is an indication of good management and a company that has the ability to sustain its profitability.

Return on Assets

It is assumed that in any business, assets exist to produce either the foundation or the means of producing, distributing, or selling a product or services. How well a company is able to leverage its assets to generate earnings from its activities is indicated by its return on assets (ROA) ratio. This ratio is calculated using the following formula:

Net income / Total assets = Return on assets

This profitability ratio uses the balance sheet for the total assets number, which is used to create a ratio that represents the relationship of net income (earnings after taxes) to the total assets of a company. Using the numbers from Mike's income statement (**TABLE 5-1**) and balance sheet (**TABLE 5-2**), the return on assets ratio is:

273,105 / 526,755 = .518 or 51.8%

In other words, each dollar of Mike's total assets is generating about 52 cents of net income. This is an indicator of how efficiently Mike's is generating income using its assets. By itself, a 52% ROA cannot be judged good, bad, or average. Cross-sectional analysis (see "Cross-Sectional Analysis" later in the chapter) must be used to compare Mike's to other bicycle retailing operations to see how Mike's stacks up to the industry averages.

TABLE 5-2: BALANCE SHEET FOR MIKE'S BIKES

Mike's Bikes
Balance Sheet December 31, 2002

Assets	
Current assets	
Cash	$160,000
Inventory	$275,000
Total current assets	$435,000
Fixed assets	
Equipment	$34,000
Buildings	$63,000
(Less accumulated depreciation)	–$5,245
Total fixed assets	$91,755
Total assets	$526,755
Liabilities and shareholder equity	
Liabilities	
Current liabilities	
Accounts payable	$20,000
Taxes payable	$83,965
Total current liabilities	$103,965
Long-term liabilities	
Long-term loans	$63,000
Total liabilities	$166,965
Shareholders' equity	
Common stock	$203,000
Retained earnings	$156,790
Total shareholders' equity	$359,790
Total liabilities and shareholders' equity	$526,755

Return on Equity (ROE)

The return on equity (ROE) ratio, which is also called return on investment (ROI) ratio or return on common equity ratio, measures earnings made possible through investment in a company, or so goes the logic behind this ratio. If you are a stockholder in a company, you are very interested in how well the company is able to generate earnings by applying the money invested in the company. The ROE ratio is calculated using the following formula:

Net income / Shareholders' equity = Return on equity

Like the ROA ratio calculation, where the balance sheet supplied the total assets amount, the ROE ratio draws on the balance sheet for the total shareholders' equity amount. The net income amount, which is the bottom line on the income statement, is divided by the total equity amount to yield the ROE ratio.

Using Mike's Bikes information from **TABLES 5-1** and **5-2**, ROE is calculated as follows:

273,105 / 359,790 = .759 or 75.9%

At face value, Mike's Bikes' ROE of 75.9% indicates that for each dollar of investment capital available to the business, it is able to generate more than 75 cents of earnings. Actually, the average ROE for most retailing operations runs between 10% and 20%, so in comparison, Mike's is very successful in terms of its return on equity.

Return on Sales Ratio (ROS)

The return on sales (ROS) ratio, widely used as a measure of a company's operational efficiency, calculates a ratio between operating income and sales. In effect, this ratio states how much operating income is generated for each dollar of sales.

Generally, the ROS is figured using earnings before interest and taxes (EBIT), also known as operating income, but occasionally the ROS is calculated using bottom-line net income after taxes. When you compare ROS between two companies, be sure you read the financial statement notes for how the ROS was calculated.

Using the more common variation, ROS is calculated using the following formula:

EBIT / Total net sales = Return on sales

Using the information from the income statement in **TABLE 5-1**, Mike's Bikes had a return on sales of 0.694, which depending on the industry averages is a seemingly good ratio. Mike's Bikes generates 69 cents of net income on each $1.00 of sales. Mike's ROS is calculated as follows:

361,165 / 520,700 = 0.694

The ROS value can help identify a company that may not be pricing its products high enough to cover its expenses or one with expenses too high for its current sales volume. It may also indicate that too many discounts are being given to customers and they are impacting profitability. Remember that some retail businesses and those in highly competitive markets may not have total control of their product pricing. In these cases, the ROS can be used to identify the effect of a company's expenses.

EBITDA

EBITDA (pronounced as "ebb-it-da") stands for Earnings Before Interest, Taxes, Depreciation, and Amortization. Sometimes you will find this number highlighted on financial statements, although it's not required. This calculated amount is used by some analysts to compare a company's financial performance to a company in a different industry. And while this number can help analyze a company's profitability, it is not in any way a measure of cash flow (even though it may be presented that way).

EDITDA is calculated using the following formula:

> **Revenue – Expenses (excluding taxes, interest, depreciation, and amortization) = EBITDA**

EBITDA should not be used to determine a company's cash flow, but it can be used as an indicator of a company's true profitability.

EBITDA emerged as a financial analysis tool during the 1980s, because it got rid of the effects of debt financing and of accounting judgments. In this way, it enables analysts to compare different companies and different industries. For example, you could better compare a manufacturing firm (which is likely to have a lot of fixed assets and a lot of debt) to a service-oriented company (which typically would have very little debt and few fixed assets). These days, EBITDA is most commonly reported in the annual reports of companies that have a lot of debt or are writing off fixed assets over longer periods of time, which can alter the looks of their earnings.

Although it can be a good tool when used properly, and in conjunction with other analysis, there are some problems with using EBITDA. Here are the primary failings of EBITDA:

- It ignores any changes in working capital and tends to overstate cash flow in periods when working capital is growing.
- It tends to be misused as a measure of a company's liquidity.
- It blurs the fact that not all of a company's revenues are cash (when being presented as representative of cash flow).
- It neglects any accounting method differences other than those used for depreciation and amortization.

However, EBITDA can be a good tool for looking at companies that have a lot of capital assets that are being depreciated extended time periods and/or companies with heavy debt burdens.

Many analysts, recognizing the shortcomings of EBITDA, recommend the use of the free cash flow (FCF) ratio as a better measurement of earnings. FCF includes three areas that EBITDA leaves out: accounts receivables, inventory, and expenditures for capital assets. Chapter 7 discusses free cash flow and its calculation in detail.

Share to Earnings Ratios

There are two primary ratios that are calculated based on the net income (earnings) of a company: the earnings per share ratio and the price to earnings ratio.

Earning per Share Ratio

As a shareholder, you want to know the amount of earnings generated by each of the shares you own—especially because this number typically is tied to dividend distributions. The earnings per share (EPS) ratio is calculated by dividing a company's earnings (net income) by the number of outstanding shares (the number of shares a company has issued that are held by shareholders). If Mike's Bikes currently has 500,000 shares outstanding, its earnings per share amount is calculated as follows:

$$\$273,105 / 500,000 = \$0.55$$

The above calculation tells us that at the end of 2002, Mike's Bikes had an EPS of $0.55. Actually, by itself the EPS doesn't tell us much. Even when compared to another firm in the same industry, there are too many other factors involved to make a good comparison. The EPS value is as dependent on the number of shares a company has issued as much as its net income for a period. As shown in **TABLE 5-3**, although the EPS ratios for the two companies are very different, their net income is the same.

TABLE 5-3: EARNINGS PER SHARE CALCULATION

	Company 1	Company 2
Net income	2,000,000	2,000,000
Shares	1,000,000	500,000
EPS	2.0	4.0

Typically, the earnings number used to calculate EPS is one of four amounts, and it's very important to know which version you're looking at:

LATEST TWELVE MONTHS (LTM): The net earnings amount from a company's year-end income statement.

TRAILING: A sum of the last four quarterly reports, which should be very close to a company's LTM earnings amount for the same time period.

FORWARD: A projection of a company's earnings for the next year.

HYBRID: A combination of the last two quarterly earnings amounts and a projection of the next two quarterly earnings amounts.

Price to Earnings Ratio

The price to earnings (P/E) ratio compares a company's current share price to its earnings per share. The P/E ratio can be used to compare a company's earnings performance for a given period, real or projected, depending on the earnings amount used (see previous section).

The P/E ratio is calculated using the following formula:

Stock price / EPS = Price to earnings ratio

What the P/E ratio attempts to answer is the amount of net earnings (income) a company is generating for each dollar of its stock price. The P/E ratio is also called the *multiple* because it can be used as an indicator of how many investors will purchase a stock and how likely they are to do so.

In the previous section, we calculated Mike's Bikes' EPS to be $0.55. If Mike's current stock price is $4.00, its P/E ratio is 7.3, which is calculated as follows:

$$\$4.00 / \$0.55 = 7.3$$

Whether a P/E ratio of 7.3, which would also be stated as 7x (7 times), is good or bad requires comparison to either a prior period's P/E ratio or comparison to other firms in the same industry. Generally speaking, though, a lower P/E ratio is a better P/E ratio.

One bit of caution on using the P/E ratio alone to judge a company's earnings performance is that some companies will buy back their stock when they aren't doing so well to make their EPS and P/E ratios look better.

Price to Earnings Growth Ratio

One of the problems in using the P/E ratio to evaluate a company as an investment opportunity is that it provides information for only the current year. There is no indication as to whether this year represents typical performance for the company or if the company has been growing. Investors that follow arbitrary rules like only investing in companies showing a certain current P/E ratio are ignoring the fact that the future could be drastically different than the present.

The very popular investment Web site, the Motley Fool (*www.fool.com*), has a rule of thumb that addresses this problem: "In a fully and fairly valued situation, a growth stock's price to earnings ratio should equal the percentage of the growth rate of its company's earnings per share."

What may appear to be an outstanding value—for example, a

good P/E ratio and a low stock price—may actually be a company that has reached its peak and will see declining earnings over the next few years before it closes its doors.

When comparing P/E ratios, you must consider the growth rates of the companies (and their industries) being considered. This means that you must consider what a company's earnings growth (expressed as a projected EPS ratio) is likely to be. Okay, I concede that the P/E ratio is a hard and fast fact and any projections we make about a company's future growth are definitely subjective, but there are ways to remove some of the guesswork from this process.

Calculating the EPS growth rate over a single year (last year to this year or even this year to next year) is easy, because the numbers required are typically available to you. The EPS growth rate calculation is calculated using the following formula:

> (Year 2 earnings – Year 1 earnings) /
> Year 1 earnings × 100 = Growth ratio

If we are able to learn that Mike's EPS ratio for 2001 was $0.49 from its Web site, and its 2002 EPS was $0.55 (see "Price to earnings ratio" earlier in the chapter), then its earnings growth rate is calculated as follows:

> (0.55 – 0.49) / 0.49 × 100 = 12.2

So, Mike's Bikes' growth rate for the years 2001/2002 is 12.2%. If Mike's management is projecting net earnings of $325,000 for 2003, this will yield a forward EPS of $0.65. The calculation of Mike's growth rate for 2002/2003 is:

> (0.65 – 0.55) / 0.55 × 100 = 18.2

So, assuming Mike's Bikes hits its earnings projection (and doesn't issue more stock), its EPS ratio will grow 18.2%, which makes the corporation appear to be a good potential investment, at least for the next year.

Another earnings performance ratio that can be used in this situation is the Price/earnings to growth ratio (PEG), which is an indicator ratio that is used to identify stocks with good growth potential. PEG is calculated as follows:

P/E ratio / Projected growth rate = Price/earnings to growth ratio

Using Mike's Bikes' numbers, we can calculate the 2002 PEG as:

7.3 / 18.2 = 0.40

The PEG ratio can be used to identify undervalued company stocks. The rule of thumb for using the PEG ratio is that companies with a PEG of less than 1 are undervalued and investors will pay less for the projected growth in the stock. Companies with a PEG ratio higher than 1 may see the same rate of growth, but investors can expect to pay more for their stock.

Price to Sales Ratio

The price to sales (P/S) ratio is often used to replace the P/E ratio when a company has negative income, which would make the P/E ratio somewhat meaningless. The P/S ratio is calculated by dividing the current stock price by the sales per share ratio, as follows:

Share price / Sales per share = Price to sales ratio

Using information from **TABLE 5-1** and the preceding sections, Mike's current stock price is $4.00 per share and its sales per share ratio for 2002 is 3.84 (2002 sales of $520,700 divided by 500,000 shares outstanding). From this we can calculate PLM's P/S ratio as follows:

$4.00 / ($520,700 / 500,000) = 3.84

As with all financial analysis ratios, you need to compare this number to other companies in Mike's industry. A lower P/S ratio indicates that an investor has the opportunity to gain the benefits of a company's revenues at a discount price. However, it may also mean that the company may be having problems converting sales to earnings or that its sales growth is below average.

Price to Book Value Ratio

A variation on the P/E ratio is the price to book value or price to book ratio (P/BV or P/B, sometimes called the price to equity ratio). The P/BV ratio is used to compare a company's share price to the company's book value per share.

A company's book value is computed from its balance sheet by subtracting total liabilities from total assets, or in other words, its shareholders' equity amount. The P/BV ratio is calculated using the following formula:

> **Share price / Book value per share = Price to book value ratio**

In 2002, Mike's Bikes, Inc. had a book value of $359,790, its current share price is $4.00, and has 500,000 shares outstanding. For 2002, Mike's P/BV ratio of 5.56 is calculated as follows:

> **$4.00 / (359,790 / 500,000) = 5.56**

At the risk of repeating myself, what constitutes a high or low P/BV varies with industry.

A relatively low P/BV ratio could mean that the stock is undervalued, making it a good deal. On the other hand, it could mean that something is fundamentally awry with the company and that flaw is reflected in a very low share price. A relatively high P/BV ratio could mean just the opposite—that the stock is overvalued on the open market, but that doesn't mean that there couldn't still be something wrong with the company. Generally speaking, however, when the rest of a company's numbers look good, a low P/BV can indicate a bargain.

Cross-Sectional Analysis

Fully employing profitability ratios to analyze a company's financial statements, especially the income statement, involves using a technique called cross-sectional analysis. Cross-sectional analysis compares the profitability ratios, and any other pertinent ratios, of several companies from the same industry. Comparing only two companies can tell you which of the two would be the better investment, but by including several companies from the same industry, you get a better picture as to which of the companies offers the best investment opportunity.

It is also much better when comparing the ratios of different companies not to place too much importance on a single or just a pair of individual ratios. You can get a much better idea as to how the companies compare when you base your comparison on several key ratios.

For example, don't pick a stock just because its earnings per share outshine that of other companies in the same industry. That ratio shows nothing about the stability, growth, and solvency of a corporation. But when looked at in conjunction with other ratios, especially ratios from different categories, you begin to see the true picture of the company behind the financial statements. When all or most of a firm's numbers look good when compared to those of its peers, then you can be more confident that your investment choice is a sound one.

Part 4

Watching Cash Flows

How money flows through a business can provide better information than the static numbers on the balance sheet and income statement. The purpose of the cash flows statement is to reconcile the cash changes that have occurred in a company during its reporting period.

I've long held the belief that if everyone did a personal cash flows statement, we'd all manage our cash a little bit better.

Chapter 6

The Cash Flows Statement

"Never ask of money spent
Where the spender thinks it went.
Nobody was ever meant
To remember or invent
What he did with every cent."

—Robert Frost

Understanding the Cash Flows Statement

What the cash flows statement (CFS), which is also referred to as the Statement of Changes in Financial Position (SCFP), provides is a reconciliation between the balance sheet and the income statement that shows the actual amounts of cash flow a company generated from its various activities in a given period. Because of the widespread use of accrual accounting methods, the balance sheet and income statements include many non-cash items that tend to distort how much actual cash a company received or paid out.

Just because a company's income statement reports millions of dollars in net income doesn't mean they actually have millions of dollars in cash. The cash flows statement consolidates information and removes the effects of accrual accounting to lift away the fog of accounting so that we can get a true picture of how much cash a company actually generates.

Even the most profitable company (as reported on its income statement) can eventually go out of business if it doesn't maintain proper cash flows to support its business. While a company can manipulate its earnings numbers, it has much less ability to manipulate its cash flow numbers, which is why the SEC requires a cash flow statement be included in their quarterly and annual reports. A cash flow statement tells it like it is—whether or not a company has cash.

Cash Flows

A cash flow is the stream of money that a company receives from its customers, lenders, and investors and spends for salaries, production materials, and other operating expenses. How much of a cash flow a business should have depends on several aspects of the business, not the least of which is its industry.

In comparison to other companies in the same industry, a company with low or negative cash flow may not be able to react in times of crisis or to take advantage of new technology being adopted by its industry.

What a Cash Flows Statement Doesn't Say

The cash flows statement is very good at telling us a company's cash position, but there are a few things it doesn't (and wasn't designed to) tell us. A cash flows statement doesn't report the details of profit or loss for the reporting period, and it doesn't provide a complete picture of the overall financial health of a company. It doesn't account for a company's assets and liabilities, just the cash involved in acquiring them.

Sure, as investors, we want to invest in companies that have positive cash flows, but even with a positive cash flow, a company still may not be a sound investment. The cash flows statement must be considered along with the income statement and the balance sheet to get a fundamental understanding of a company at a given point in time.

Tracking the Source and Use of Money

Contrary to what Robert Frost may think (see the quote at the beginning of this chapter), the cash flows statement *is* meant to report exactly where the money went, along with what exactly provided it in the first place. Where the balance sheet reports the status of a company's assets, liabilities, and equity and the income statement reports the operational elements that contributed to a company's profit or loss, the cash flows statement follows the money, the actual dollars, through the company to show how cash was used by the company during the reporting period.

For business management, the value of the cash flows statement is that it can provide operational information that helps to determine when and if the company may need to take out a loan or look for additional investments.

Why Track Cash Flows?

The Financial Accounting Standards Board (FASB—pronounced "faz-bee") established the requirement that a cash flows statement be included in a company's financial statements in 1988. It was believed then that, because of accrual accounting methods, a company's management could make a variety of decisions that would have an impact on the valuations reported on the balance sheet and income statement; a belief that is still true today.

Accrual accounting requires companies to make judgments about such things as whether or not to have a reserve account for uncollectible or bad debts, the useful life of certain assets over which depreciation is calculated, how long to carry accounts receivables and accounts payable, when to actually book (record) a sale, and much more. Each of these judgments have a bearing on how net income is determined and reported—but they have no direct impact on cash.

Cash flows statements are less likely to be impacted by a

company's accounting decisions because they deal with the actual sources and uses of cash money as it has flowed (or will flow, in a cash flow projection statement) through the business. Investors and analysts often use the discounted present value of a company's projected cash flows to determine the company's value. Creditors use cash flows to determine a company's ability to pay (with cash) its debts. Even profitable companies can have cash flow problems, which in turn could create debt payment problems.

The Cash Flows Statement

A cash flows statement is divided into three sections: cash flows from operating activities, cash flows from investing activities, and cash flows from financing activities, in that order (see **TABLE 6-1**). Not every company necessarily has cash flows to report from all three areas, but for the most part, companies have some cash flows from at least two.

TABLE 6-1: A SAMPLE CASH FLOWS STATEMENT USING THE INDIRECT METHOD

Ronprico Enterprises, Inc.
Cash Flows Statement for the Year Ending 12/31/02

Cash Flows from Operating Activities	
Net income	$30,903
Depreciation expense	$3,133
Increase in accounts receivable	$(9,225)
Decrease in inventory	$15,357
Decrease in prepaid expenses	$2,500
Increase in accounts payable	$5,453
Increase in accrued expenses	$4,428
Decrease in interest payable	$(4,725)
Decrease in income taxes payable	$(2,500)
Total cash flow from operating activities	$45,324

Cash Flows from Investing	
Purchase of property and equipment	$(12,300)
Total cash flow from investing	$(12,300)
Cash Flows from Financing	
Increase in long-term debt	$22,451
Issuance of capital stock	$26,638
Dividend payments	$(4,000)
Total cash flow from financing	$45,089
Net increase in cash	$78,113
Cash at beginning of year	$120,000
Cash at end of year	$198,113

Cash Flows Statement Methods

FASB set two distinct methods for formatting a cash flow statement: direct and indirect. The difference between the two methods is in the cash flows from the operating activities section of the statement. The other two sections of the cash flows statement, investing activities and financing activities, are the same in either method.

The more commonly used indirect method begins with net income (from the income statement of the same period) and makes adjustments for items that don't directly affect cash flow, effectively reconciling net income with cash (as shown in **TABLE 6-1**). Using the direct method, information about cash collections and cash payments with vendors and employees is included in the operating activities section (as shown in **TABLE 6-2**). Whichever presentation method is used, the resultant cash flows from operations will be the same.

The following sections discuss each of the sections on the cash flows statement in more detail.

Cash Flows from Operating Activities

A company's operating activities are those directly related to the production and delivery of goods and services to its customers. The cash flows from operating activities section of the statement can be formatted in one of two ways, either direct or indirect. The operating activities section of the direct method cash flows statement looks at a company's operating activities in the same sequence they are listed on the income statement, collections (revenue) first and payments (expenses) second.

Regardless of the format, this section of the cash flows statement includes the ongoing and regular activities that are related to the production and delivery of a company's goods and services to its customers. This includes:

- Changes in current assets (not including cash) and liabilities.
- Cash received for operating activities, such as customer payments and interest and dividend revenue (which sound like they should belong in the investing activities section, but under the FASB guidelines are included in the operating activities section).
- Cash payments made by the company to support its operating activities, including payments to suppliers and employees, payments for operating expenses (such as rent, utilities, and supplies), interest payments, and any taxes paid during the period.

Cash Flows from Operating Activities—Direct Method

The cash flows from operating activities using the direct method has five major entries: cash collections, cash payments, cash generated from operations, interest paid, and income taxes paid. Any extraordinary cash flows, such as insurance claim proceeds, would be listed separately within this section. **TABLE 6-2** shows a sample operating activities section formatted using the direct method.

TABLE 6-2: A SAMPLE CASH FLOWS
FROM OPERATING ACTIVITIES SECTION
USING THE DIRECT METHOD

Ronprico Enterprises, Inc.
Cash Flows Statement (excerpt) for the Year Ending 12/31/02

Cash Flows from Operating Activities—Direct Method	
Cash collections	$89,933
Cash payments for purchases	$(27,521)
Cash payments for operating expenses	$(9,863)
Cash payments for interest	$(4,725)
Cash payments for income taxes	$(2,500)
Total cash payments	$(44,609)
Net cash provided by operating activities	$45,324

Cash Collections

The first entry in the cash receipts area is cash received from customers, which includes any cash received (the accountants love to call this cash collected) from customers and any others who paid money to the company for sales in the normal course of operations.

The cash collections entry includes both cash sales and the cash received from credit sales (also known as on-account sales). The cash collections from credit sales amount is calculated using the following formula:

(Beginning accounts receivable + Credit sales) – Ending accounts receivable = Cash collections from credit sales

To calculate the cash received from credit sales we need to add the credit sales recorded during the reporting period to the accounts receivable balance at the beginning of the period, and then subtract the end of period accounts receivable balance.

For example, Ronprico Enterprises began the year with $61,233 in accounts receivable, and had $51,200 in credit sales plus $46,000 in cash sales during the year. The company ended the year with an accounts receivable balance of $68,500. For this company, the cash collections from credit sales amount is $43,933. This amount is calculated as follows:

$$(61,233 + 51,200) - 68,500 = 43,933$$

The amount of cash received from cash sales (which includes all sales paid for immediately by the customer, whether by cash, check, or credit card) is then added to the cash collections from credit sales and the sum equals the cash collections for the period, which is entered into the cash flows statement.

So, to the cash collections from credit sales we add the company's cash sales receipts of $46,000, which results in total cash collections for the period of $89,933, as shown in **TABLE 6-2**. Cash collections are recorded in the operating activities section as a positive (source) amount.

Cash Payments

Throughout the operating year (or whatever the reporting period may be), purchases are made for materials that go into the production of a product (in manufacturing companies) and for inventory (in retail companies). In addition, cash payments are paid for the day to day operating expenses of the business.

To calculate the cash payments made for purchases entry, the process is virtually the same as that used for cash collections (see preceding section). Purchases for production materials are typically made on some sort of credit terms, which adds the invoice amount for each purchase to the accounts payable balance. Cash payments for purchases is calculated using the following formula:

$$\text{(Beginning accounts payable + purchases)} - \text{Ending accounts payable} = \text{Cash payments for purchases}$$

For example, if the company had a beginning accounts payable balance of $22,331, purchased $34,300 of materials during the year, and ended the year with an accounts payable balance of $29,110, their cash payments to vendors entry should be $27,521. This is calculated as follows:

$$(22,331 + 34,300) - 29,110 = 27,521$$

Any direct cash purchases for inventory and production materials, although atypical, should also be added, although this is not a common business practice. The cash payments for purchases entry is recorded in the operating activities section as a negative (use) amount.

Cash Payments to Operating Expenses

The cash payments for operating expenses includes such things as salaries and wages paid to employees (usually the biggest operating expense) and everyday bills like rent, utilities, and Internet access. This entry is calculated using the same method as used for the cash payments for purchases entry. The operating expenses actually paid during the period are added to any accrued expenses at the beginning of the period and the accrued expenses ending balance is then subtracted, as shown in this formula:

(Beginning accrued expenses + operating expenses) – Ending accrued expenses = Cash payments for operating expenses

If a company had $10,063 in accrued expenses at the beginning of the period, paid an additional $12,800 in expenses during the period, and ended the period with an accrued expense balance of $13,000, the company's cash payments for operating expenses entry should be $9,863, which is computed as follows:

$$(10,063 + 12,800) - 13,000 = 9,863$$

The cash payments for operating expenses amount is entered in the operating activities section as a negative (use) amount.

Cash Flows from Operating Activities

The net amount that results from subtracting the total cash payments (which includes the payments described above plus payments made for interest and income taxes) from the cash collections entry represents the cash flow amount from operating activities during the period. This sum should be a positive amount if the company is pricing its products to provide some margin of profits. If the cash from operating activities amount is negative, it should raise a red flag that something is not right with the company's operating activities.

Cash Flows from Operating Activities— Indirect Method

The more commonly used alternative for preparing the operating activities section of the cash flows statement is the indirect method. The primary difference between the direct method and the indirect method is where they start, since they both end up at the same place. While the direct method starts at the top of the income statement to track the cash collections and cash payments and arrive at the net operating cash flow, the indirect method starts at the bottom line with net income from the income statement and reconciles it to the cash flows from operations. **TABLE 6-3** shows a cash flows from operating activities section prepared using the indirect method.

TABLE 6-3: A SAMPLE CASH FLOWS FROM OPERATING ACTIVITIES SECTION USING THE INDIRECT METHOD

Ronprico Enterprises, Inc.
Cash Flows Statement (excerpt) for the Year Ending 12/31/02

Cash Flow from Operating Activities—Indirect Method	
Net income	$30,903
Depreciation expense	$3,133
Increase in accounts receivable	$(9,225)
Decrease in inventory	$15,357
Decrease in prepaid expenses	$2,500
Increase in accounts payable	$5,453
Increase in accrued expenses	$4,428
Decrease in interest payable	$(4,725)
Decrease in income taxes payable	$(2,500)
Total cash flow from operating activities	$45,324

Net Income Reconciliation

The first entry in the indirect method form of an operating activities section is the net income amount from the income statement for the same period.

The net income amount is then adjusted for non-cash expenses or gains that reduce or increase income, but that aren't the result of a cash receipt or payment flow. For example, depreciation, which reduces income on the income statement, is an expense item that does not involve a cash flow. So depreciation, a non-cash expense, is added back to the net income. Other examples of the adjustments made to net income are the net changes in accounts receivable, inventory, and prepaid expenses, which are all non-cash assets, and the net changes in the balances of liabilities accounts like accounts payable, accrued expenses, and income taxes.

The premise behind these adjustments is to convert accrual basis accounting to cash basis accounting so the readers of the financial statements can see the movement of cash throughout the reporting period. Changes in current asset accounts (other than cash) and current liability accounts affect cash flows. For example, when a current liability has decreased over the year, that means that cash was used to pay it down. On the other hand, an increase in a current liability account means that cash payment was put off, which adds to the cash availability in the current period.

Cash Flows from Investing Activities

The investing activities of a company involve purchasing and selling non-current assets, such as buildings, machinery, equipment, and buying and selling stocks and bonds issued by other companies or organizations. **TABLE 6-4** shows the cash flows from investing section for Ronprico Enterprises.

The cash flows normally included in the investing activities section are the inflows from such activities as the sale of assets, the sale of a portion of a business, and the sales of stock and bonds (issued by other companies). The cash outflows included in the investing activities section include payments made for purchases of property, plant, and equipment, the purchase of a new business unit, or the purchase of the stocks and bonds of other companies.

TABLE 6-4: A CASH FLOWS FROM INVESTING ACTIVITIES SECTION OF A CASH FLOWS STATEMENT

Cash Flows from Investing Activities	
Purchase of property and equipment	$(12,300)
Total cash flow from investing activities	$(12,300)

Changes to current assets and liabilities were accounted for in the operating activities section of the cash flow statement, but the investing activities section deals only with changes to non-current assets. Be aware, though, that what one company considers a fixed asset, another may consider a current asset, as described in the following example.

For example, ABC Machinery, which is in the business of selling large industrial equipment, buys a large forklift for use in moving equipment around its warehouse. This purchase would appear in the investing activities section of the company's cash flows statement. But on the cash flows statement of XYZ Forklifts, that sale would appear in the operating activities section of its cash flows statement, since it was a normal sale of inventory made in the normal course of operations.

Cash Flows from Financing Activities

The financing activities section of the cash flows statement includes any transactions that involve the sale or buy-back of a company's own stock and bonds, any dividend payments made to its shareholders, and any changes in non-current liabilities or shareholders' equity. **TABLE 6-5** shows the financing activities section of Ronprico Enterprises' cash flows statement.

The cash inflows typically included in the financing activities section are from issuing stock or borrowing by issuing a bond or signing a note. The cash outflows included in this section come from a company buying back its own stock or bonds, repaying a loan, paying off a lease, or paying out dividends to its shareholders.

TABLE 6-5: THE FINANCING ACTIVITIES SECTION OF A CASH FLOWS STATEMENT

Cash Flows from Financing Activities	
Increase in long-term debt	$22,451
Issuance of capital stock	$26,638
Dividend payments	$(4,000)
Total cash flow from financing	$45,089

Buying and selling of stocks and bonds that were issued by another company is included in the investing section of the cash flows statement. However, when a company issues or buys back its own stock or bonds, the cash flows are included in the financing section.

Let's clear up the biggest areas of confusion: dividends and interest. Dividends paid out to shareholders are included in the financing section, but any interest paid to bondholders is included in the operating activities section. Any dividend or interest payments received by a company are included in the cash flows from operating activities section of its cash flows statement.

The Cash Flows Statement Summary Lines

The bottom of the cash flows statement may be the part most people read first. Typically, a few lines (see **TABLE 6-6**) are used to provide a reconciliation of the cash flows statement and to summarize the operating, investing, and financing sections of the statement. The most common entries are:

- **NET INCREASE IN CASH:** This entry provides a net total of the three sections of the cash flows statement. (If the total is negative, this entry is called net decrease in cash.)
- **CASH AT THE BEGINNING OF THE PERIOD:** This entry provides the total cash balance at the beginning of the reporting period of the cash flows statement.
- **CASH AT THE END OF THE PERIOD:** This entry should be the sum of the net increase in cash and the cash at the beginning of the period amounts. This number must equal the cash balance reported on the balance sheet for the period ending date.

**TABLE 6-6: THE SUMMARY LINES
ON A CASH FLOWS STATEMENT**

Net increase in cash	$78,113
Cash at beginning of period	<u>$120,000</u>
Cash at end of period	$198,113

Summary

The cash flows statement is only one piece of the financial analysis puzzle. While it provides a look at the cash position of a company at a given point in time, it doesn't include much of the information detailed on the income statement and the balance sheet.

Chapter 7 explains the processes used to analyze a cash flows statement and how it ties back to the other statements required by the SEC and defined by the FASB standards.

Analyzing Cash Flows

*"Finance is the art of passing currency from
hand to hand until it finally disappears."*

—Robert W. Sarnoff

The Importance of Cash Flow

Cash flow is the lifeblood of any business. In fact, most experts argue that a strong cash flow is more important to the success of a business than its ability to produce and deliver goods and services to customers. Their argument is that customer service can always be improved, but a company that doesn't have the cash to pay its suppliers, lenders, or employees is likely out of business. The importance of a healthy cash flow to a business can't be overemphasized.

Profits versus Cash Flows

Another important concept to understanding cash flows is that profits and cash flow are completely different. Where profit only considers income and expenses for a specific time period, such as a month, quarter, or year, cash flow is concerned with the movement of money into and out of a business. Profits are impressive to show on an income statement, but a positive cash flow on a cash flows statement is even more impressive. Remember that even a profitable company can go bankrupt by neglecting and disregarding its cash flow; unlikely, but possible.

QRS Sales has a very good sales month and books sales of $250,000. If QRS's cost of sales is $200,000, it should realize a $50,000 (20%) gross profit. However, if most of the sales are made to a single customer, who is very slow to pay or perhaps files for bankruptcy 60 days later, QRS may not have enough cash flow to pay its accounts payable and may need to borrow or liquidate some assets to cover its cash flow shortfall.

The Value of the Cash Flows Statement

The most commonly used financial analysis liquidity ratios, the current ratio and the quick ratio, are based on information taken from the balance sheet (see Chapter 3). The limitation of the information used in the balance sheet liquidity ratios is that the amounts available represent only a fixed point in time (typically, the end of an accounting period). In contrast, the cash flows statement reports the changes that have occurred between succeeding balance sheets without the distortions of accrual accounting conventions. The important information shareholders need in regard to cash flow, primarily cash flows from operations and investments, is on the cash flows statement.

However, the balance sheet does have some valuable information when it comes to analyzing a company's cash flow management, as explained in the next section.

Cash Flow Indicators

Successful companies do experience cash flow problems from time to time, but those that have learned to manage their cash flow have the best chances of survival and prosperity. Although this chapter is about analyzing a cash flows statement, the balance sheet can also provide some insight into how well a company is managing its cash flow.

A few of the key elements to look for to identify a company with what appears to be sound cash flow management (or not) are:

ACCOUNTS RECEIVABLE: The number of days of accounts receivable a company is carrying can be an indicator of good or bad cash flow. A company's days receivable ratio (see Chapter 3) should be compared to its days payable ratio along with its industry averages to determine if the company has possible cash flow problems.

ACCOUNTS PAYABLE: The number of days of accounts payable a company carries can also indicate either good or bad cash flow management. If the company's days payable ratio (see Chapter 3) is significantly lower than its days receivable ratio, a cash flow shortfall may be looming. However, if the days payable ratio is higher, the company is funding its accounts payable (providing the amounts are nearly equal) with customer payments.

INVENTORY: If a company's inventory is growing faster than its sales, it's possible that too much of its cash is being converted into excess inventory, which, in most cases, is a cash flow no-no. However, a single year of inventory growth may not be a predictor of future cash flow problems. The company may be purchasing extra inventory to take advantage of special quantity discounts, paying its accounts payables faster than normal to take trade (payment) discounts, or building up a new product to be put into production in the near future.

Cash flow gaps are virtually unavoidable at times for any business, especially seasonal businesses. A company may have cash flow gaps during its slower season that are filled in during its busy season. In these cases, a company may need to carry lines of credit, bank loans, or extended accounts payable agreements with its suppliers to smooth out its cash flow.

Cash Flow Ratios

A company's cash flows statement is an important resource for information about a company's liquidity. Cash flows statements are often overlooked as information sources by investors who prefer to examine and analyze balance sheets and income statements. However, two important ratios can be calculated from the information on the cash flows statement (drawing on the other statements as well) that provide insight into a company's cash flow management and its liquidity: the operating cash flow ratio and the cash current debt coverage ratio.

> Like all financial analysis ratios, the ratios discussed in this chapter are best used when they are compared to the ratios of other companies in a business's industry. The cash flow of a cash-only street vendor may look incredible against a large multi-division manufacturing firm, but perhaps not so hot against other street vendors. What is good or normal in one industry isn't always the same in different industries.

Operating Cash Flow Ratio

The operating cash flow (OCF) ratio is a measure of a company's ability to cover its current liabilities through its cash flow from operations. The OCF ratio is calculated using the following formula:

> Cash flows from operations / Current liabilities =
> Operating cash flow ratio

The cash flows from operations amount is found on the cash flows statement and the current liabilities amount is found on the balance sheet.

The OCF ratio measures how well a company's operations generate enough of a cash flow to meet its current liabilities. If the OCF ratio is 1.0 or better, the company is generating sufficient cash flows from operations to pay its current debts. If the OCF ratio is below

1.0, the company will likely need to find other cash sources to fund its operating activities or slow down its payments to its creditors. Other cash sources include existing cash and/or cash equivalents that can be applied to cover the cash flow gap. However, if this condition is ongoing, the existing cash sources probably won't last too long, and the company could be forced to find other sources for cash, such as through financing activities (borrowing).

For example, using the statement of cash flows for Ronprico Industries (see **TABLE 7-1**), which indicates $45,324 in cash flow from operations, we can calculate an OCF ratio, assuming the current liabilities from the company's balance sheet are $39,235, as follows:

$$45,324 / 39,235 = 1.16$$

Ronprico's OCF ratio of 1.16 indicates that the company's operational activities are generating enough cash flow to cover its current liabilities.

TABLE 7-1: A SAMPLE CASH FLOWS STATEMENT

Ronprico Enterprises, Inc.
Cash Flows Statement for the Year Ending 12/31/02

Cash Flow from Operating Activities	
Net income	$30,903
Depreciation expense	$3,133
Increase in accounts receivable	$(9,225)
Decrease in inventory	$15,357
Decrease in prepaid expenses	$2,500
Increase in accounts payable	$5,453
Increase in accrued expenses	$4,428
Decrease in interest payable	$(4,725)
Decrease in income taxes payable	$(2,500)
Total cash flow from operating activities	$45,324

TABLE 7-1: A SAMPLE CASH FLOWS
STATEMENT (CONTINUED)

Ronprico Enterprises, Inc.
Cash Flows Statement for the Year Ending 12/31/02

Cash Flow from Investing	
Purchase of property and equipment	$(12,300)
Total cash flow from investing	$(12,300)
Cash Flow from Financing	
Increase in long-term debt	$22,451
Issuance of capital stock	$26,638
Dividend payments	$(4,000)
Total cash flow from financing	$45,089
Net increase in cash	$78,113
Cash at beginning of year	$120,000
Cash at end of year	$198,113

Cash Current Debt Coverage Ratio

The cash current debt coverage (CCD) ratio is used to measure a company's ability to repay its current debt through its cash flow from operations. This ratio is different from the OCF ratio in that cash flow from operations is adjusted by the amount of the cash flow that will be paid as dividends. This is done by subtracting the amount of any cash dividends paid, found in the cash flows from financing activities section of the cash flows statement.

The current debt amount used as the denominator in this ratio is the portion of current liabilities (from the balance sheet) that is interest-bearing, that is the current debt on which a company pays interest. Any amount for interest payable is not included in the current debt amount, only current liability payments on which interest is charged.

The CCD ratio is calculated using the following formula:

> (Cash flows from operations – Cash dividends) / Current interest-bearing debt = Cash current debt coverage ratio

If the CCD ratio for a company is less than 1.0, the company's operating activities are not generating sufficient cash flow to cover its current debt liabilities after dividend payments are made to shareholders. A CCD ratio of 1.0 or higher indicates that a company's operating activities are generating enough cash to cover its current debt.

Ronprico Enterprises lists $25,000 of current interest-bearing debt on its balance sheet, which means its CCD ratio is calculated as follows:

> (45,324 – 4,000) / 25,000 = 1.65

Since its CCD ratio is well above 1.0, Ronprico's operating activities are generating enough cash to cover its current debt obligations after paying dividends to its shareholders. Since Ronprico also had an OCF ratio above 1.0, it appears it has healthy cash flows from operating activities to cover all of its current liabilities.

Debt to Cash Flow Ratio

Where the CCD ratio measures how well the operating activities are generating cash to cover current debt, the debt to cash flow (DCF) ratio measures the company's overall cash flow and its ability to cover all of the company's debt (current and long-term). Debt to cash flow ratio is calculated using the following formula:

> Total debt / Total cash flows = Debt to cash flow ratio

The debt to cash flow ratio essentially determines approximately how many years it should take a company to pay off its total debt at the current cash flow level. For example, if Ronprico currently has a total of current and long-term debt of $300,000, using its total cash flows of $78,113 (see **TABLE 7-1**), we can calculate its DCF ratio as follows:

$$300,000 / 78,113 = 3.84$$

So, at its current cash flow levels, Ronprico theoretically should be able to pay off its total outstanding debt in 3.84 years. In essence, if the DCF ratio is 1.0 or lower, all of a company's debt can be considered current debt (although it may actually be long-term debt by contractual agreement). The lower the DCF ratio, the better the company is able to cover its debt through its cash flows.

Cash Interest Coverage Ratio

The cash interest coverage (CIC) ratio measures how well cash flows are able to cover cash payments made for interest on interest-bearing debt. This ratio is somewhat akin to the times interest earned ratio (also called the interest coverage ratio) associated with the income statement (see Chapter 5), but it addresses the issue that interest payments are paid with cash and not profits.

The CIC ratio is calculated by dividing the cash flow from operating activities, which includes any cash payments for interest and income taxes, by the cash payments for interest, using the following formula:

$$\text{Cash flow from operations} / \text{Interest payments} = \text{Cash interest coverage ratio}$$

Ronprico Enterprises's cash flows statement shows cash flows from operations of $45,234, including interest payments of $4,725. Its CIC ratio is calculated as follows:

$$45,324 / 4,725 = 9.59$$

A CIC ratio of 9.59 indicates that Ronprico is generating nearly 10 times as much cash as it requires to pay its interest obligations. Obviously, the lower this ratio is for a company, the more you need to be concerned about its ability to meet its interest-bearing debt obligations.

Capital Expenditure Ratio

The capital expenditure (CE) ratio measures the cash flow available for future investment and for payments on existing debt. This ratio is calculated by dividing a company's cash flow from operating activities minus dividends paid by any payments made for fixed assets, such as buildings and equipment. A CE ratio greater than 1.0 indicates that a company is able to cover its capital investments with its cash flows, with money still available to pay its debts and fund future expansion.

The CE ratio is calculated using the following formula:

(Cash flow from operations – Dividends) / Fixed asset payments = Capital expenditure ratio

TABLE 7-2 shows a portion of the Ronprico Enterprises cash flows statement that indicates cash flows from operations are $45,324, dividend payments of $4,000, and investments in property and equipment of $12,300. Ronprico's CE ratio is calculated as follows:

(45,324 – 4,000) / 12,300 = 3.36

A CE ratio of 3.36 indicates that Ronprico has more than sufficient cash flow to continue to invest in plant and equipment and cover its debt obligations.

TABLE 7-2: A PORTION OF A CASH FLOWS STATEMENT

Total cash flow from operating activities	$45,324
Cash Flow from Investing	
Property and equipment	$(12,300)
Total cash flow from investing	$(12,300)
Cash Flow from Financing	
Long-term debt	$22,451
Capital stock	$26,638
Dividend payments	$(4,000)
Total cash flow from financing	$45,089

Price to Cash Flow Ratio

The price to cash flow ratio is a bit of a departure from the other cash flow ratios we have been looking at, but it can be a good measure of a company's worth as an investment. A relatively high price to cash flow ratio (in comparison to other firms in a company's industry) is an indication that the stock market has a corresponding positive outlook on the company's future financial stability. The price to cash flow ratio along with the price to earnings (P/E) ratio provide indications of a stock's relative value.

Cash Flow per Share

The first step in determining the price to cash flow ratio is to compute the cash flow per share (CFPS), which is calculated using the following formula:

> Cash flow from operations / Shares outstanding =
> Cash flow per share

The cash flow per share is calculated by dividing the cash flow from operating activities by a company's number of common shares outstanding. On its own, the cash flow per share is another indicator of a company's financial strength.

Ronprico Enterprises has $45,324 of operating cash flow and 100,000 shares outstanding, so its cash flow per share is calculated as:

$$45,324 / 100,000 = 0.45$$

In this case, the company has 45 cents of cash flow per share. Whether that is good or bad depends on the average for its industry and the investor's perception when comparing this ratio to other companies. However, as we discussed earlier, an indication of low cash flows should be an early warning that a company may have trouble meeting all of its financial obligations, including paying dividends, going forward.

Price to Cash Flow Ratio

The price to cash flow ratio is calculated using the following formula:

Current share price / Cash flow per share = Price to cash flow ratio

For example, if Ronprico's stock is currently trading at $4.25, its price to cash flow ratio is 9.44, which is calculated as follows:

$$4.25 / 0.45 = 9.44$$

In general, a lower price to cash flow ratio indicates a stock price that is relatively properly priced. In other words, a higher price to cash flow ratio can indicate a stock that is overvalued against the cash flows being generated by a company. Remember that ratios are also called *multiples*.

The price to cash flow ratio is used a couple of different ways by the financial world. A company with a low price to cash flow ratio (in comparison to other companies in its industry) may be an acquisition target by a larger company. Investors may eliminate companies that have a price to cash flow ratio of 10.0 or more, companies that aren't generating sufficient cash flows, as investment candidates. The price to cash flow ratio, when used in combination with the price to earnings ratio, can be used to identify companies that have both good cash flow and good earnings.

Cash Flow Growth Ratio

Another indication of a financially strong company is its operating cash flow growth, or the rate of change in its operating cash flow from year to year. Cash flow growth is calculated using the following formula:

> (Year 2 cash flow − Year 1 cash flow) / Year 1 cash flow =
> Cash flow growth ratio

Although the above formula implies that cash flow growth is calculated between years, it can also be calculated for any two time periods, such as quarterly, monthly, etc. In the cash flow growth formula given above, "Year 2" represents the cash flow from the current or latest period and "Year 1" represents the cash flow from the earlier or previous period.

If Ronprico Enterprises experienced $38,000 of cash flow in a prior year and $45,324 in the current year, the cash flow growth ratio is calculated as follows:

> (45,324 − 38,000) / 38,000 = 0.19 or 19%

The benchmark in Ronprico's industry for the cash flow growth ratio is 20%, but this ratio varies widely from industry to industy. Like all other ratios, what is or isn't a good growth rate can only be determined through comparison to the average cash flow growth rate of a company's industry.

Free Cash Flow

Free cash flow is the cash left over after all of the obligations of a company are met. Virtually every company is in business to generate as much free cash flow as possible. Free cash is the cash flow from operating activities minus any capital equipment expenditures and dividends paid (found on the cash flows statement), using the following formula:

> Operating cash flow − (Capital expenditures + Dividends paid) =
> Free cash flow

It should be noted that free cash flow is not a ratio, but a dollar amount that represents the amount of free cash available.

TABLE 7-3 shows the portion of the Ronprico Enterprises cash flows statement needed to calculate its free cash flow. From its total operating cash flow of $45,324, we subtract the property and equipment expenditures of $12,300 and dividend payments of $4,000, which yields free cash of $29,024, as follows:

> 45,324 − (12,300 + 4,000) = 29,024

TABLE 7-3: PORTION OF A CASH FLOWS STATEMENT

Total operating cash flow	$45,324
Cash Flow from Investing	
Property and equipment	$(12,300)
Total cash flow from investing	$(12,300)
Cash Flow from Financing	
Long-term debt	$22,451
Capital stock	$26,638
Dividend payments	$(4,000)
Total cash flow from financing	$45,089

The Importance of Free Cash Flow

The one truly important aspect of free cash flow is that it drives share prices higher. A company that has a positive free cash flow is very solvent, profitable, and usually pays dividends, all desirable characteristics of a company in which most investors want to invest.

Free cash flow is a somewhat rare commodity among publicly held companies. In fact, because it has become so coveted by investors, many financial statements now highlight their cash flows in order to have investors believe them to have free cash flows.

In 2001, General Electric was listed as being the company with the most free cash flow, over $19 billion, by an investment research firm in an edition of *BusinessWeek* magazine.

Technically, the net capital spending amount used in the calculation of free cash flow should be only that used to maintain the existing facilities and equipment and should not include any new investments in capital assets. But, unless you are a good estimator, have a good inside contact at a company, or have access to interview corporate management, in most cases, net capital spending is used as listed on the cash flows statement. In calculating free cash flows for each of the nearly 8,000 stocks in its database, Morningstar assumes that all capital spending is necessary (maintenance) spending.

For more information about Morningstar and its services, visit *www.morningstar.com*.

Investors generally should look for companies that have good free cash flow growth and/or companies with good free cash flow per share and a relatively low stock price (as indicated by a good price to free cash flow ratio, explained next).

Free Cash Flow per Share Ratio

To calculate a company's free cash flow per share ratio, assuming you have already calculated its free cash flow, you divide the company's free cash flow by the company's number of outstanding shares, using the following formula:

Free cash flow / Shares outstanding = Free cash flow per share ratio

Ronprico Enterprises has $29,024 in free cash flow (calculated above) and has 100,000 shares outstanding, so its free cash flow per share ratio is 0.29, which is calculated as follows:

29,024 / 100,000 = 0.29

A free cash flow per share of 0.29 translates to 29 cents per share of free cash flow.

Price to Free Cash Flow Ratio

The next step in looking at free cash flow is the price to free cash flow ratio, which measures the relative value of a company's stock in terms of the company's free cash flow. This ratio is calculated using the following formula:

Current share price / Free cash flow per share =
Price to free cash flow ratio

If the current share price of Ronprico's stock is $4.25, then its price to free cash flow ratio is 14.66, which is calculated as follows:

4.25 / 0.29 = 14.66

Based on the free cash flows of the company, its stock is overvalued. If this were an actual company, you might want to wait for the share price to drop before buying the stock.

Working Capital and Free Cash

As discussed in Chapter 2, working capital is current assets minus current liabilities, as reported on the balance sheet of a company. The cash flows statement measures and quantifies any changes in these categories. **TABLE 7-4** shows how changes on the balance sheet are reflected in changes on the cash flows statement.

TABLE 7-4: BALANCE SHEET CHANGES AND THEIR IMPACT ON THE CASH FLOWS STATEMENT

Change on Balance Sheet	Change on Cash Flows Statement
Current assets (other than cash) increase	Operating cash flow decreases
Current assets (other than cash) decrease	Operating cash flow increases
Current liabilities increase	Operating cash flow increase
Current liabilities decrease	Operating cash flow decreases

Flow Ratio

A ratio that addresses these changes in working capital as a part of the free cash flow analysis, made popular by the Motley Fools (Tom and David Gardner), on their *www.fool.com* Web site, is the flow ratio. This ratio estimates the ability of less-liquid assets to pay the current liabilities on which a company typically doesn't pay interest.

The first step in calculating the flow ratio is to subtract cash and cash equivalents, accounts receivable, and easily marketable securities from current assets (summed up as cash and near-cash), resulting in a value that in essence represents inventory and prepaid expenses. Inventory represents products to be sold in the future; prepaid expenses are just what they sound like—expenses paid in advance (like insurance).

Next, short-term interest-bearing debt is subtracted from current liabilities, resulting in a value that includes accounts payable, accrued expenses, and other current debts—obligations on which a company typically doesn't pay interest. Actually, companies with the right cash flow can make money on these liabilities because they can leave the money in the bank drawing interest until the bills have to be paid.

The formula for calculating the flow ratio is:

Current assets – [Cash + Near-cash assets] / (Current liabilities – Short-term interest-bearing debt) = Flow ratio

Let's call the numerator of this ratio "inventory and other current assets," because that's what remains after we take out the cash and cash equivalents and other near-cash assets. We'll call the denominator "payables and other current liabilities," using the same logic.

All of this information is easily found on the balance sheet. The balance sheet is used instead of the cash flows statement for the flow ratio because the amounts used are more easily found there.

TABLE 7-5 shows an excerpt from a sample company's balance sheet listing the entries we need to calculate the flow ratio.

TABLE 7-5: AN EXCERPT FROM A
SAMPLE BALANCE SHEET

Current assets	
Cash and equivalents	$240,000
Inventory	$1,800,000
Other current assets	$175,000
Total current assets	$2,215,000
Current liabilities	
Accounts payable	$750,000
Notes payable	$600,000
Accrued expenses and other current liabilities	$157,000
Total current liabilities	$1,507,000

Using the information in **TABLE 7-5**, we can calculate a flows ratio for this company by dividing its inventory and other current assets by its accounts payable and other current liabilities, as follows:

$$(2,215,000 - 240,000) / (1,507,000 - 750,000) = \text{Flow Ratio}$$

$$1,975,000 / 757,000 = 2.61$$

Most analysts are looking for a target flow ratio close to 1.5, which represents a good balance between liabilities and inventory. Not every company nor every industry can achieve the 1.5 flow ratio goal because there could be special requirements and circumstances which would prevent it, such as seasonal inventory buildup, new product launches, or the like. However, any company that can achieve a 1.5 balance between its inventory and liabilities is moving stuff out of the warehouse into the hands of customers and managing its liability payments.

A 2.61 flow ratio tells us that this company may not be turning over its inventory as fast as it should, or its inventory has grown too large for its level of operating activities. To reach a flow ratio in the range of 1.5, this company would need to reduce its inventory by 50% (to around $900,000). Of course, it could also raise its accounts payable, but that is hardly moving in the right direction financially. One of the benefits of reducing inventory is that it usually reduces accounts payable.

Looking into Dot-Com Cash Flows

There are a pair of cash flow ratios that can be applied to just about any company, but have been especially useful in analyzing the cash flows of telecommunication and Internet companies: the cash burn rate and the days of expenses ratios.

Cash Burn Rate Ratio

High-tech start-up companies, such as a company with Internet-related services or products, typically require some lead-time before they can put their product online. During this lead-time, how much cash the company is using can be very telling about its chances of actually launching its products before it requires additional funding.

The cash burn rate ratio is calculated by dividing a company's operating expenses (minus amortization and depreciation expenses) by the number of days in a period, typically 360 for a year. The formula for the cash burn rate ratio is:

Operating expenses (less depreciation and amortization) / 360 = Cash burn rate

For example, if a start-up company has $1,200,000 in operating expenses (not including depreciation and amortization) on its period-end financial statements, its cash burn rate is calculated as follows:

$1,200,000 / 360 = 3,333

In this example, the company is spending, or burning through, over $3,000 per day. Whether that rate is good or bad depends on how much cash the company has left and how much more time it needs before the product is ready for sale.

Days of Expenses Ratio

Another cash burn rate ratio is the days of expenses ratio. This ratio indicates the number of days at a company's current cash burn rate that the company will exhaust its net assets (current assets – current liabilities). The formula for the days of expenses ratio is:

(Current assets – Current liabilities) / Cash burn rate = Days of expenses ratio

For example, if a company has net assets of $540,000 and a cash burn rate of $3,333, its days of expenses ratio is calculated as follows:

$$\$540,000 / \$3,333 = 162.0$$

At its current cash burn rate, this company has assets to cover about 162 days of operations before it exhausts its assets and must seek additional funding.

Chapter 8

How Others Use Financial Statements

"Acquaintance, n.: A person whom we know well enough to borrow from, but not well enough to lend to."

—Ambrose Bierce

In the Eye of the Beholder

Once a company publishes its financial statements publicly they are subject to analysis and interpretation by whomever wishes to do so. A publicly held corporation has little control over the opinions gleaned by others about their financial situation based on the information the company publishes to the world.

Financial statements are published to a variety of audiences: government officials (like the Securities Exchange Commission [SEC]); bankers and other lenders; shareholders, owners, and potential investors; company management; labor leaders; and, of course, financial analysts. Each of these groups looks at the same information, but may (and usually do) interpret it differently.

GOVERNMENT OFFICIALS: Governments are typically concerned about whether a company's annual report complies with the reporting and valuation regulations and whether taxable income has been properly computed.

135

BANKERS AND OTHER LENDERS: Bankers are concerned with a company's cash flow and short-term liquidity ratios, such as the current and quick ratios. Bondholders are looking for long-term solvency indications. And all current and future lenders want to see low leverage ratios, such as the debt to assets ratios.

SHAREHOLDERS, OWNERS, AND POTENTIAL INVESTORS: In general, this group is looking for profitability and high dividend payouts. Stock speculators looking for growth stocks to purchase are more concerned with the growth ratios, like the earnings growth ratio, and such things as free cash flow, which indicate an ability to grow.

COMPANY MANAGEMENT: Inside managers use financial statements for performance comparisons using the various ratios to diagnose possible business problems that require action. For example, a purchasing agent may focus on inventory turnover; an accountant may concentrate on the accounts receivable turnover ratio to determine if the company's credit policies need correction; and the board of directors may scrutinize the company's overall profitability.

LABOR LEADERS: A labor union official pays special attention to any potential source of wage increases and the funding of the company's pension plan.

FINANCIAL ANALYSTS: This group, depending on their industry specialization, looks at all of the above, plus the big picture—the overall financial health of the company.

In this chapter, we will look at the two primary reviews performed on financial statements: the banker's review as a part of analyzing a loan application and the analysis performed by financial analysts.

Apples and Oranges

Problems occur when comparing the financial statements of one company to another, especially companies in different industries. The source of the incomparability of financial statements stems from the fact that companies tend to use differing accounting methods, and the differences occur in some fairly major financial statement categories.

Different accounting methods make comparing two or more companies' financial statements difficult, especially in five major financial statement categories:

CAPITALIZATION/EXPENSE: A company may either capitalize (treat as an asset) or expense certain costs, such as leases and natural resource rights.

COMMON STOCK INVESTMENTS: Some companies value common stock at cost or market; others value their common stock investments at their equity value.

DEPRECIATION: A company can legally use a variety of depreciation methods. Some companies may use straight-line depreciation and others a declining-balance or a sum-of-the-years digit method.

DISCONTINUED OPERATIONS AND EXTRAORDINARY ITEMS: This area is open to interpretation and definition by each individual company. The FASB does provide some guidance in this area but, by and large, a company can use its discretion as to what and how items are included in this section.

INVENTORY VALUATION: One company may value its inventory using FIFO, another using LIFO, and yet another using a weighted average scheme.

On top of the above areas, another area where companies can differ is how they value and list intangible assets. The value and potential worth of patents, copyrights, trademarks, and especially goodwill, are strictly open to interpretation.

Cooking the Books

In addition to the above potential incompatibilities, anyone analyzing a company's financial statements must also consider the fact that on occasion financial statements reflect managerial decisions that can distort the true current financial status of a company.

For example, if a company writes-down its asset value to reduce its future depreciation and amortization expenses, that could alter its current equity value. (The write-down reduces current net income and shows up in the equity section through the retained earnings amount.) Reducing discretionary costs (such as advertising, maintenance, and training expenses) can increase a company's current net income, but can have a negative long-term impact on its ability to generate future earnings. Inventory purchases can be delayed until after the end of the fiscal year or the accounts payable balance can be paid down prior to year-end to increase a company's current ratio.

These actions can improve the look of the financial statements for a single year, but will show up when more than one year's reports are analyzed. I can think of no better reason to compare a company's financials for more than a single year than this.

Sources of Information

Virtually every financial statement, at least those of mid- to large-size companies, contains notes, which are also occasionally called footnotes. Two kinds of footnotes are used on financial statements:

ACCOUNTING POLICIES: Accounting policy notes identify and explain the accounting methods and practices of a company, such as its inventory valuation method, its depreciation method, and other major accounting method applications.

DISCLOSURES: Although typically very legalistically worded, disclosure notes provide details on long-term debt, stock options, pension plans, corrections to previous errors in the financial statements, internal controls (or the lack thereof), and any litigation in which the company is currently involved.

It should be noted that although FASB requires certain note disclosures, there are no hard and fast standards for how notes are formatted. Beyond those required by FASB, just how concisely or clearly a financial statement's notes are worded is really up to the company writing them.

How Bankers Use Financial Statements

By and large, bankers will not loan money to a company that does not submit financial statements. Bankers are in the money business and without the financial track record of a company, most are not willing to take a chance on making a bad loan.

Most bankers have no preference for how a company values its inventory or depreciates its assets, as long as these accounting methods are applied consistently. In fact, consistency is the key characteristic most bankers are looking for: consistency in profitability, consistency in generating revenue, consistency in managing costs, and consistency in applying accounting methods.

Applying for a Loan

The primary reason a company submits its financial statements to a bank is to obtain a loan. When a bank's loan committee looks over a company's loan application, there are five major considerations:

1. **ABILITY TO REPAY THE LOAN:** Not surprisingly, this is the first consideration. The sources of this information are the company's income statement and cash flows statement.
2. **BALANCE SHEET CONDITION:** The balance sheet ratios are used to determine a company's liquidity and solvency.

3. **COLLATERAL:** The bank looks both for collateral on the company's balance sheet and that the collateral is free of encumbrances.
4. **MANAGEMENT:** What are the experience, qualifications, and track record of the company's management team?
5. **TRENDS:** Also considered are the trends in the company's industry, the company's potential for developing new products or markets, and its prospects for the future.

Bankers prefer to review a spread of historical financial statements from a company, which indicates the company's ability to repay a loan. If the financial statements do not reflect consistent positive performance by the company, collateral becomes an issue.

Questions Bankers Ask

A small company applying for a bank loan can expect to answer a series of questions. Here are some of the questions a company should be ready to answer:

- Has the business existed for at least three years?
- Has the business filed bankruptcy in the past 10 years?
- What is the business's days payable ratio?
- Is the business currently involved in any litigation?
- Has the business been profitable for at least the past two years?
- What are the business's cash flow ratios?

The Five Cs of Bank Credit

Banks tend to base their lending decisions on what they call the Five Cs of Credit:

CHARACTER: What are the experience, qualifications, and track record of the company's management, and does the company pay its obligations on time?

CREDIT: Does the company have credit references, and is it creditworthy?

CASH FLOW: Most banks are cash flow lenders, which means they look at the cash flow of a business as its primary means of repaying a loan.

CAPACITY: Does the business have the ability to generate the amount of net income required or the ability to convert assets to cash to pay an additional debt obligation?

COLLATERAL: While banks make both secured and unsecured loans, they always prefer secured debts.

How Analysts Use Financial Statements

Financial or stock market analysts use several types of analysis to determine the value of a company's stock. The primary two methods used however, are fundamental analysis and technical analysis.

Fundamental Analysis

As I stated earlier in the book, a company's financial statements can provide a wealth of information, if you only know how to find it. That is the underlying principle of fundamental analysis, which uses what is called quantitative analysis to find the gold in the financial statement mine.

Fundamental analysis reviews the historical performance of a company to predict its future performance. An analyst performing fundamental analysis on a company wants as much information as possible concerning the company's assets, liabilities, revenue, expenses, cash flows, and all other financial information. Of secondary interest in this analysis is the company's current stock price.

The preferred fundamental/quantitative analysis tool used by what are called "value analysts" is the price to earnings (P/E) ratios. The P/E ratios are indicators of a stock's value and value analysts attempt to evaluate the whole stock market using composite P/E ratio indexes. In contrast to value analysts are "growth analysts," who focus more on a company's future earnings than its current income levels.

Fundamental analysts distill information about a company into four categories from its financial statements:

PROFITABILITY: This category uses the profitability ratios, such as ROA and profit margin, to develop a profit-potential profile of a company.

EARNINGS: This category of information tracks both the past and projected earnings of a company.

FUNDAMENTAL RATIOS: This category includes the quantitative analysis ratios for a company, such as P/E, price to sales, etc.

VALUATION: This category provides an assessment of the value of a company's stock using several per share ratios.

Technical Analysis

You may have heard of the Dow-Jones Index, but did you know that Charles Dow (the Dow of Dow-Jones), who was the first editor of the *Wall Street Journal*, is considered the father of technical analysis?

Tracking stocks using indexes is at the heart of technical analysis, and Dow developed stock indexing as a way to identify trends that could be used as guidelines for investing. Dow's first two indexes, back in 1897, included 12 industrial stocks in one index and 20 railroad stocks in the other. The idea was that the closing price trends for the industrial stocks, which produce products, would be confirmed by the railroad (companies that transport goods) index. To technical analysts, the stock price, especially a stock's closing price, is everything.

On Your Own

Now that we've felled the financial statements monster and turned on the lights, it's not so scary. With the weapons in this book, you can successfully attack and dissect even the most complex-looking reports. Instead of looking at the pretty pictures, you'll flip straight to the footnotes to learn about the company's accounting practices. Rather than reading the chairman's rah-rah report, you'll whip out your calculator and compute some ratios.

And what will you do with all this newfound knowledge? You'll invest in stocks that make sense for your financial plan. If you're looking for growth, you'll want to check out profitability and growth ratios and the company's free cash flow. If you want stability and dividend checks, look at the dividend payouts and analyze the company's solvency.

Perhaps the most important thing we've discussed is the fact that you should not look only at a single number, statement, ratio, or company. You need to perform a variety of computations on each of the big three financial statements (balance sheet, income statement, and cash flows statement). You need to look at more than just one company in the industry, and check out the industry averages as well.

You must not focus on only the easy-to-find figures that are highlighted by the corporation—they want you to see the positive and overlook the negative. You have to look beyond the obvious. Yes, you'll need a calculator and a block of time. But the results will be well worth it.

A

ACCELERATED COST RECOVERY SYSTEM (ACRS): A depreciation rates schedule used for income tax purposes.

ACCOUNTANT'S OPINION: A signed statement made by an independent public accountant that he (or his public accounting firm) has reviewed a company's records and accounts. The statement may be either qualified or unqualified. A qualified statement cites certain exceptions the accountant has noted, and an unqualified statement attests to no exceptions found.

ACCOUNTING EARNINGS: The earnings amount reported on a company's income statement.

ACCOUNTING INSOLVENCY: A financial condition where a company's total liabilities exceeds its total assets, which means the company has a negative net worth and is insolvent according to its accounting records.

ACCOUNTING LIQUIDITY: The ability to convert assets to cash quickly and easily.

ACCOUNTS PAYABLE: The account that tracks money owed to suppliers, vendors, and (in some cases) employees.

ACCOUNTS RECEIVABLE: The account that tracks money owed to a company by its customers.

ACCOUNTS RECEIVABLE AGING: A listing of each customer's account by invoice due date used to determine which customers are late paying and to alert management to potential problems with its collection processes.

ACCOUNTS RECEIVABLE TURNOVER: A ratio of net credit sales to the average accounts receivable balance that can be used as a measure of how quickly a company's customers are paying.

ACCRUAL BASIS: The accounting practice that records expenses and income when they are incurred or earned, regardless of whether cash has been paid or received.

ACID TEST RATIO: A ratio that measures a company's liquidity and its ability to meet its obligations. This ratio is calculated by dividing current assets, less inventory and prepaid expenses, by current liabilities. This ratio is also called the quick ratio.

ACQUISITION: The action when a company purchases assets, such as factories, equipment, or all or part of another company.

ACQUISITION COST: The total cost of purchasing an asset and getting it ready for use, including sales tax, freight charges, and installation. If the asset acquired is all or part of another company, the total would include legal and closing costs. When purchasing stock, this term refers to the price of the stock plus brokerage fees.

ACRS: See *accelerated cost recovery system*.

AGING: See *accounts receivable aging.*

ADMINISTRATIVE EXPENSES: The typical daily costs (other than cost of goods sold) incurred by a company, such as for office salaries, paper clips, and phone bills.

AMORTIZATION: The allocation of the periodic cost of an intangible asset over its beneficial life.

ANNUAL REPORT: A report of financial condition produced at the end of a company's fiscal year that includes a description of the company's operations and its financial statements: balance sheet, income statement, statement of cash flows, and perhaps others. Publicly traded companies are required by the SEC to produce and distribute annual reports.

APPRECIATION: The amount an asset increases in value.

ASSET: Any physical or intellectual property owned by a company that is expected to benefit future operations.

ASSET ACTIVITY RATIOS: A set of ratios, often referred to as return on investment ratios, used to measure how effectively a company is managing its assets.

ASSET CLASSES: Categories of assets grouped for reporting and accounting purposes, such as plant, equipment, and real estate all lumped together as "fixed assets."

ASSET TO EQUITY RATIO: The ratio between total assets and shareholders' equity, which indicates the portion of assets actually owned by the company.

ASSET TURNOVER: The ratio between net sales and total assets, which indicates how well existing assets are being used to produce sales.

ASSET VALUE: The net market value of a company's assets, typically calculated on a per share basis.

ASSETS: See *asset*.

AUDITOR'S REPORT: See *accountant's opinion*.

AVERAGE AGE OF ACCOUNTS RECEIVABLE: A weighted-average aging of a company's outstanding customer invoices.

AVERAGE COLLECTION PERIOD: The ratio that measures the number of days a company must wait to receive payment for credit sales. Also called days receivables.

B

BALANCE SHEET: A summary statement of a company's assets, liabilities, and shareholders' equity on which total assets must equal total liabilities plus shareholders' equity. This statement is sometimes referred to as the statement of financial condition.

BANKRUPTCY: The condition in which a company is unable to pay its debts and seeks legal protection from its creditors.

BOND: A debt obligation for more than one year issued by a company, typically sold on the open market. The issuing company agrees to repay the principal amount of the bond at a specified time. Some bonds are also interest-bearing and the selling company pays periodic interest to the bondholders.

BOOK VALUE: The value of a company computed by subtracting its total liabilities from its total assets.

BOOK VALUE PER SHARE: A ratio calculated by dividing a company's book value by the number of its outstanding shares. This ratio measures a company's historical accounting value, as opposed to its current market value, on a per share basis.

BUSINESS FAILURE: The condition that exists when a company has ceased operations without paying its creditors.

BUY-BACK: The action when a company repurchases some or all of its outstanding shares from shareholders. These bought-back shares are listed as treasury stock in the equity section of the balance sheet.

C

CAPITAL: Money that has been invested in a company.

CAPITAL ASSET: An asset, such as land or equipment, with a useful life longer than three years that is used in the normal course of business but not held for resale.

CAPITAL EXPENDITURES: Money spent to acquire or improve capital assets.

CAPITAL GAIN: The amount realized when an asset, such as stock, building, or land, is sold for more than its current book value.

CAPITAL GOODS: See *capital asset*.

CAPITAL LEASE: An equipment or building lease that must be included on the balance sheet of the lessee as both an asset (the property leased) and a liability (the total value of the lease) as if the lessee owned the property.

CAPITAL LOSS: The result produced when an asset, such as stock, building, or land, is sold for less than its current book value.

CAPITAL TURNOVER: A ratio calculated by dividing a company's net sales by its shareholders' equity that measures the efficiency of a company's capital investments.

CAPITALIZATION: The amount of long-term debt and equity used to fund a company's assets.

CAPITALIZATION RATIOS: Ratios used to measure a company's debt to total capitalization or the extent that a company is leveraging its equity.

CASH: The monetary value of assets that are convertible into cash immediately, such as demand bank accounts, actual cash on hand, and undeposited checks from customers. See also *cash equivalents*.

CASH ASSET RATIO: A liquidity ratio that is calculated by dividing a company's cash and marketable securities by its current liabilities. See also *liquidity ratios*.

CASH BASIS ACCOUNTING: The accounting method that recognizes and records revenues and expenses only when cash is actually received or paid out.

CASH EARNINGS: A company's cash revenues minus its cash expenses.

CASH EQUIVALENTS: Assets that can be converted into cash immediately or that mature within 90 days. Cash equivalents include such things as certificates of deposit (CDs) and easily marketable securities.

CASH FLOW: The movement of cash into and out of a business through its operations, investing activities, and financing activities.

CASH FLOW COVERAGE RATIO: A ratio that measures how many times a company's financial obligation is covered by its earnings before interest, taxes, depreciation, and amortization (EBITDA). See also *earnings before interest, taxes, depreciation, and amortization*.

CASH FLOW FROM OPERATING ACTIVITIES: The amount of a company's net cash flow resulting from its normal operations.

CASH FLOW PER SHARE: A ratio that measures a company's cash flow from operating activities minus any preferred stock dividends paid out, divided by the number of its outstanding shares.

CASH FLOWS STATEMENT: A standard financial report that reconciles the cash flows in and out of a business from a company's operating, financing, and investing activities and reports its change in financial position.

CASH RATIO: A ratio that compares a company's cash to its current liabilities.

CERTIFIED FINANCIAL STATEMENTS: A company's financial statements that include an accountant's opinion. See also *accountant's opinion*.

CERTIFIED PUBLIC ACCOUNTANT (CPA): A licensed accountant who has met a state's certification standards, such as testing and experience.

COLLECTION RATIO: The ratio that measures the number of days a company must wait to receive payment for credit sales. This ratio is also referred to as days receivables and average collection period.

COMMON SHARES: Units of stock issued by a corporation which entitle the holder to attend and vote at shareholders' meetings and receive discretionary dividends from the company.

COMMON STOCK: See *common shares*.

COMPANY: An enterprise that engages in commerce and business, which may be formed as either a proprietorship, partnership, or corporation.

COMPETITION: The contention among companies each trying to control a larger share of a market.

CONSUMER GOODS: Goods and services purchased for personal use and not used in production, such as food, clothing, entertainment, and the like.

CONTRA ACCOUNT: An account whose balance is deducted from an associated account in financial statements.

CORPORATION: A legal business entity that is created as a separate legal person under the law, effectively separating ownership from management. A corporation may own assets, incur liabilities, and buy and sell securities.

COST BASIS: The method of accounting for an asset using its original acquisition cost. See also *acquisition cost.*

COST OF GOODS SOLD: The cost of raw materials and all other direct expenses incurred to produce or purchase a product or service held for resale. This is sometimes called cost of sales.

COVERAGE RATIOS: A set of ratios that measure the ability of earnings to cover debt obligations. These ratios are also called solvency ratios.

CREDIT: The generic term used to describe money loaned to a company.

CURRENCY: Money issued by a government that is a medium of exchange, a legal tender, and a store of value.

CURRENT ASSETS: The value of a company's cash, accounts receivable, inventory, securities, and other assets that can be converted into cash in less than one year or one operating cycle.

CURRENT LIABILITIES: The value of a company's obligations for accounts payable, salaries, interest, and other debts that are due within one year.

CURRENT RATIO: A ratio that measures a company's ability to pay its short-term debts that is calculated by dividing its current assets by its current liabilities.

D

DAYS RECEIVABLES: The ratio that measures the number of days a company must wait to receive payment for credit sales. This ratio is also referred to as average collection period.

DAYS SALES IN INVENTORY RATIO: A ratio that measures the average number of days it takes to sell inventory.

DEBT: A generic term used to describe money borrowed and owed by a company.

DEBT RATIO: A ratio that measures a company's total debt to its total assets, calculated by dividing total debt by total assets.

DEBT TO EQUITY RATIO: A ratio that measures how leveraged a company is to its shareholders' equity. This ratio is calculated by dividing total liabilities by shareholders' equity.

DEPRECIATE: The process of allocating the acquisition cost of an asset over its useful life.

DEPRECIATION: The non-cash expense incurred by depreciating an asset. See also *depreciate*.

DIVIDEND: A discretionary payment made to a company's shareholders from its net income.

DIVIDEND PAYOUT RATIO: The percentage of net income a company pays out to its shareholders as dividends. See also *dividend*.

DIVIDENDS PAYABLE: The dollar amount of dividends a company has declared to be paid out to shareholders but has not yet paid.

E

EARNINGS: A company's net income from an accounting period.

EARNINGS BEFORE INTEREST AFTER TAXES (EBIAT): The financial subtotal that shows revenues minus only cost of goods sold, operating expenses, and income taxes, disregarding interest.

EARNINGS BEFORE INTEREST AND TAXES (EBIT): The financial subtotal that shows revenues minus cost of goods sold, depreciation, and operating expenses, disregarding income taxes and interest.

EARNINGS BEFORE INTEREST, TAXES, AND DEPRECIATION (EBITD): The financial subtotal that states revenues less cost of goods sold and operating expenses, excluding depreciation, and disregarding interest and income taxes.

EARNINGS BEFORE INTEREST, TAXES, DEPRECIATION, AND AMORTIZA-TION (EBITDA): The financial subtotal that states revenues minus cost of goods sold and operating expenses, excluding depreciation and amortization, and disregarding interest and income taxes.

EARNINGS PER SHARE (EPS): A multiple that measures a company's net profit on a per share basis. EPS is calculated by dividing net earnings by the number of outstanding shares.

EARNINGS-PRICE RATIO: See *price to earnings ratio.*

EBIAT: See *earnings before interest after taxes.*

EBIT: See *earnings before interest and taxes.*

EBITD: See *earnings before interest, taxes, and depreciation.*

EBITDA: See *earnings before interest, taxes, depreciation, and amortization.*

EBT: See *earnings before taxes.*

EPS: See *earnings per share.*

EQUITY: The amount that represents the value of ownership's interest in a company.

EQUITY MULTIPLIER: A ratio that measures the value of a company's total assets to each dollar of shareholders' equity, also called the asset to equity ratio.

F

FASB: See *Financial Accounting Standards Board.*

FEDERAL RESERVE SYSTEM: The monetary agency of the U. S. government that regulates monetary policy and supervises member banks, bank holding companies, and the foreign branches of U. S. banks.

FIFO: See *first in/first out.*

FINANCIAL ACCOUNTING STANDARDS BOARD: The most important accounting body which develops and issues rules on acceptable accounting practices.

FINANCIAL ANALYSIS: The process used to analyze a company's financial statements.

FINANCIAL ANALYST: Typically an employee of a brokerage or management company who studies companies for the purpose of making buy or sell recommendations about a company's stock. Most analysts specialize in a specific industry.

FINANCIAL LEVERAGE: The use of debt to improve the return on equity.

FINANCIAL LEVERAGE RATIOS: A set of ratios, such as the debt to equity ratio, used to analyze the indebtedness of a company. These ratios are also known as solvency ratios.

FINANCIAL POSITION: The financial status of a business as reported on its financial statements.

FINANCIAL RATIO: The numerical value created by dividing one financial statement value by another.

FIRST IN/FIRST OUT (FIFO): An inventory accounting valuation method that uses the cost of the most recent purchases to value inventory.

FISCAL YEAR: An accounting period of 12 consecutive months. A fiscal year doesn't necessarily need to coincide with a calendar year.

FIXED ASSET: Any asset that has a useful life of three years or more. Fixed assets are physical such as buildings, machinery, and equipment.

FIXED ASSET TURNOVER RATIO: A ratio that compares a company's sales to its net fixed asset value. This ratio measures how efficiently those assets are used to produce sales.

FIXED COST: A cost that remains constant for a given number of production units and a fixed time period.

FREE CASH FLOWS: The net cash flows from operations minus dividends and net capital expenditures. This is the cash flow that is available for reinvestment and expansion.

G

GAAP: See *generally accepted accounting principles.*

GENERALLY ACCEPTED ACCOUNTING PRINCIPLES (GAAP): The rules and procedures that define the guidelines for acceptable accounting practices in the United States.

GOODWILL: Based on a company's acceptance or high esteem in the market, this is a value over and above a company's book value that could be obtained if the company were sold.

GROSS PROFIT: Net revenues minus cost of goods sold.

GROSS PROFIT MARGIN: A ratio that measures a company's gross profit against its revenues.

GROSS REVENUE: The total of all revenue sources before customer discounts and returns are deducted.

GROWTH RATE: The percentage change in a particular financial statement value over a period of time.

I

INCOME STATEMENT: This financial statement shows revenues, expenses, and net income for a company over a particular time period. It is also called a statement of operations.

INCOME TAX: The tax levy placed on a company by a local, state, or federal government based on its adjusted earnings.

INDUSTRY: The general business affiliation of a company based on its products or services.

INFLATION: The percentage rate that the general price level of goods and services rises from one year to the next.

INSOLVENT: Having liabilities that exceed assets.

INTANGIBLE ASSET: A non-physical asset, such as goodwill, intellectual property, patents, copyrights, and the like.

INTEREST: The fee paid over and above a borrowed amount as the expense of borrowing money.

INTEREST COVERAGE RATIO: A ratio that compares a company's earnings before interest and taxes (EBIT) to its annual interest expense to measure its ability to pay interest charges. See also *earnings before interest and taxes.*

INTEREST EXPENSE: The money paid out by a company for interest on borrowed funds.

INVENTORY: The raw materials, work in progress, and goods available for sale held by company.

INVENTORY TURNOVER: A ratio that measures the number of times a company completely uses up and/or sells its inventory and replenishes it.

INVESTMENT: An opportunity to generate money using capital.

INVESTMENT INCOME: The revenue realized from a company's investments.

INVOICE: A bill created by a seller requesting payment from a purchaser for goods or services delivered by the seller to the purchaser.

L

LEASEHOLD IMPROVEMENT: An improvement made by a company to a leased asset.

LEVERAGE: The use of debt financing as a part of a company's capital strategy.

LEVERAGE RATIOS: Ratios that measure a company's indebtedness and its ability to pay financing charges.

LEVERAGED COMPANY: A company that has incurred debt to finance its operations.

LIABILITY: A financial obligation made by a company to pay a specific amount of money or provide a service at a specific time.

LIQUID ASSET: An asset that can be quickly and easily converted to cash.

LIQUIDITY: A financial condition in which a company holds liquid assets in excess of its liabilities.

LIQUIDITY RATIOS: A set of ratios that measure a company's ability to pay its short-term liabilities.

LONG-TERM: An accounting term that indicates a period of one year or longer.

LONG-TERM ASSETS: Fixed or intangible assets with useful service lives of at least three years.

LONG-TERM DEBT: A financial obligation that is not due for more than one year.

LONG-TERM LIABILITIES: See *long-term debt.*

LOSS: The excess of expenses over revenues; negative net income.

M

MACRS: See *modified accelerated cost recovery system.*

MARKET-BOOK RATIO: A ratio that measures the price of a company's stock to the book value per share of the company. This is also called price to book ratio.

MODIFIED ACCELERATED COST RECOVERY SYSTEM (MACRS): A depreciation rates schedule used for income tax purposes.

MULTIPLE: A term commonly used by financial analysts to mean price/earnings ratio, usually stated as "the multiple."

MULTIPLES: See *ratios.*

N

NET ASSETS: The difference between total assets and total liabilities.

NET INCOME: The excess of a company's total revenues over its costs of doing business, including cost of goods sold, operating expenses, interest, income taxes, and other expenses. Also called "the bottom line."

NET INCOME PER SHARE: *See earnings per share.*

NET MARGIN: A ratio that compares a company's net income to its net revenues.

NET REVENUES: Total gross sales less any returns and discounts granted to customers.

NET WORKING CAPITAL: The difference between current assets and current liabilities.

NET WORTH: The amount represented by shareholders' equity.

NOT-FOR-PROFIT: An organization created to perform charitable, humanitarian, or educational activities in which no one participates in profits or losses.

NOTE: A debt obligation with a maturity date over one year in the future, but less than ten years in the future.

O

OBLIGATION: A legal responsibility to act, such as to repay a loan or pay an invoice.

OPERATING CASH FLOW: The flows of cash into and out of a business from its normal operations. Operating cash flow differs from earnings in that earnings may include such things as orders for which a payment has not yet been received and such non-cash items as depreciation and amortization expenses.

OPERATING MARGIN: A ratio that compares a company's operating profit to its net sales to measure the company's operating efficiency.

OPERATING PROFIT (OR LOSS): Revenues from operating activities less operating costs and expenses.

OUTSTANDING SHARES: The number of shares issued by a company, currently held by outside shareholders.

OVERHEAD: The general expenses of a company that are not directly related to the production of a good or service.

OWNER'S EQUITY: The amount of invested capital plus retained earnings.

P

PAID-IN CAPITAL: The investment in a corporation over and above the stated par value of its stock.

PATENT: An exclusive right to produce or sell a particularly unique product or process without competition for a designated period.

PAYABLES: See *accounts payable*.

P/E RATIO: See *price to earnings ratio*.

PREFERRED STOCK: Non-voting shares in a company that gives the holder a priority claim against assets and earnings in the event of a liquidation. Typically, preferred stock is paid a fixed dividend that is paid out before common share dividends are paid.

PREPAID EXPENSES: An asset account that includes any operating expense amounts paid in advance, such as insurance.

PRICE TO BOOK RATIO: A ratio that measures a company's current share price to its book value per share.

PRICE TO EARNINGS RATIO: A ratio that measures a company's current share price to its earning per share ratio.

PROFIT: The positive amount left over when costs and expenses are subtracted from revenues.

PROFIT MARGIN: A ratio that compares a company's net income (profit) to its net revenues.

PROFITABILITY RATIOS: A set of ratios that measure a company's ability to generate profits.

PUBLICLY HELD: A company whose stock is available for purchase by any individuals or institutions.

Q

QUICK ASSETS: The value of current assets minus inventory and pre-paid expenses.

QUICK RATIO: A ratio that measures a company's liquidity and its ability to meet its obligations. This ratio is calculated by dividing current assets, less inventory and prepaid expenses, by current liabilities. This ratio is also called the acid test ratio.

R

RATIO: A calculation in which two values are compared to one another.

RATIO ANALYSIS: A financial analysis technique that uses ratio calculations.

RAW MATERIALS: The basic materials a manufacturer converts into a salable product.

RECEIVABLES TURNOVER RATIO: A ratio that measures a company's ability to manage its accounts receivable. It is calculated by dividing total net operating revenue by the average value of accounts receivable.

RESERVE: An amount set aside for a contingency liability.

RETAINED EARNINGS: Earnings not paid out as dividends and held by the company for purposes of reinvestment.

RETAINED EARNINGS STATEMENT: A financial statement that details the transactions affecting a company's retained earnings account.

RETURN ON ASSETS (ROA): A ratio that measures a company's profitability and efficiency. ROA is calculated by dividing net income by total assets.

RETURN ON EQUITY (ROE): A ratio that measures a company's profitability and efficiency. ROE is calculated by dividing net income by shareholders' equity.

S

SELLING EXPENSES: Costs associated with the sale of a product, such as advertising and sales commissions.

SHARE: A certificate (or equivalent) that represents a unit of ownership in a corporation.

SHAREHOLDER: A person or institution that owns at least one share in a company.

SHAREHOLDERS' EQUITY: A company's net worth, which is the net amount of a company's total assets minus its total liabilities.

SHORT-TERM: Any financial obligation or investment with a maturity of one year or less.

SHORT-TERM DEBT: A liability that must be paid within the next 12 months.

SOLVENCY: The financial condition where a company's assets are greater than its liabilities, which results in the company being able to meet its obligations.

STATEMENT OF CASH FLOWS: A financial statement that reconciles a company's cash receipts and payments during a specific period.

STATEMENT OF CHANGES IN FINANCIAL POSITION: See *statement of cash flows.*

SUBSIDIARY: A company that is wholly or partially owned by another company.

T

TANGIBLE ASSET: A physical asset, such as a building, production machinery, or office furniture.

TAX LIABILITY: The amount in taxes a taxpayer owes to a federal, state, or local taxing authority (government).

TAXABLE INCOME: Gross profit less a variety of deductions.

TIMES INTEREST EARNED RATIO: A ratio that measures a company's ability to pay interest payments. This ratio is calculated by dividing earnings before interest and taxes (EBIT) by interest expense. See also *earnings before interest and taxes.*

TOTAL REVENUE: The sum of all sources of revenue in a period.

W

WORKING CAPITAL: The difference between current assets and current liabilities.

WORKING CAPITAL RATIO: A ratio that measures working capital against total assets.

WRITE-DOWN: A reduction in the book value of an asset.

WRITE-OFF: The accounting process that transfers all or a portion of an asset's value to expense, such as depreciating or amortizing the asset value.

Ratios Used in Financial Analysis

"Get your facts first, and then you can distort them as much as you please."

—Mark Twain

This appendix brings together all of the ratios I have included in this book in one place, plus a few more that you may hear analysts mention. I have organized these financial ratios first according to the financial statement with which each is most normally associated (although there is some overlap for a few), then in alphabetical order by the ratio name.

Balance Sheet Ratios

The ratios and formulas included in this section are used to analyze the information found on a balance sheet. I have included a sample calculation with each ratio or formula using the information in **TABLE B-1**.

Balance Sheet Principle

The underlying principle of the balance sheet is summarized in the following formula:

Assets = Liabilities + Shareholders' equity

For the balance sheet in **TABLE B-1**, the total asset value for 2002, as calculated through assets and equity is:

$$526,360 = 224,836 + 301,524$$

TABLE B-1: BALANCE SHEET
As of December 31

	2002	2001
Assets		
Current assets		
Cash	$93,378	$62,639
Accounts receivable	$95,689	$87,800
Inventory	$127,352	$130,162
Total current assets	$316,419	$280,601
Fixed assets	$201,476	$172,493
Other assets	$8,465	$6,617
Total assets	$526,360	$459,711
Liabilities		
Current liabilities:		
Accounts payable	$96,590	$107,492
Short-term debt	$24,148	$26,873
Total current liabilities	$120,738	$134,365
Long-term debt	$84,504	$86,317
Other liabilities	$19,594	$17,098
Total liabilities	$224,836	$237,780
Equity		
Common stock	$150,000	$150,000
Retained earnings	$151,524	$71,931
Total equity	$301,524	$221,931
Total liabilities and equity	$526,360	$459,711

Cash Ratio

One liquidity ratio is the cash ratio, which calculates a ratio between a company's cash balances and its current liabilities. The cash ratio is calculated using the following formula:

Cash / Total current liabilities = Cash ratio

The company in **TABLE B-1** has a 2002 cash balance of $93,378, so its cash ratio is calculated as follows:

93,378 / 120,738 = 0.77

A cash ratio of 0.77 indicates that the company has enough cash on hand to cover about 77% of its current liabilities.

Current Ratio

A company's current ratio is an indicator of how well it can pay its current liabilities with its current assets.

The current ratio is calculated using this formula:

Current assets / Current liabilities = Current ratio

For example, using the numbers from **TABLE B-1**, the current ratio is calculated as:

316,419 / 120,738 = 2.62

A current ratio of 2.62 says that this company has enough current assets to cover the obligation of its current liabilities.

Days Payable Ratio

The days payable ratio is calculated using the following formula:

Days in period / Payable turnover = Days payable ratio

Using the payable turnover calculated later in this appendix, we can calculate the company's days payable ratio as follows:

360 / 8.36 = 43.06

The standard trade credit terms are 30 days in most industries. A days payable ratio over 40 indicates that the company is holding onto its payables until after their due dates to pay its invoices.

Days Receivable Ratio

The days receivable ratio indicates how fast or slow a company's customers pay their bills and is calculated using this formula:

Days in period / Receivables turnover ratio = Days receivable

Assuming the company's receivables turnover ratio is 15.31 (as calculated below), its days receivable ratio is calculated as:

360 / 15.31 = 23.51 days

A days receivable ratio of 23.51 indicates that customers are paying invoices within one month of receiving them. If the company gives its customers the standard 30 days to pay, we can conclude that the company is managing its receivables well.

Debt to Assets Ratio

The debt to assets (D/A) ratio is used to determine what percentage of a business's assets has been funded through debt. The D/A ratio is calculated using the following formula:

Total liabilities / Total assets = Debt to assets ratio

Using the information in **TABLE B-1**, the debt to assets ratio is calculated as follows:

224,836 / 526,360 = 0.43

For most industries, a debt to asset ratio of 0.50 or less is considered good. A higher D/A ratio may indicate an overleveraged company.

Debt to Equity Ratio

The D/E ratio measures the amount of debt a company is carrying as a percentage of its shareholders' equity. The D/E ratio is calculated using the following formula:

Total liabilities / Shareholders' equity = Debt to equity ratio

Using the information from **TABLE B-1**, the D/E ratio is calculated as follows:

224,836 / 301,524 = 0.75

A D/E ratio of 0.75 indicates the company has sufficient equity to cover its debts. Most analysts look for a leverage ratio of less than 1.0, meaning that there is enough net worth in the business to cover its liabilities. This ratio is sometimes called the leverage ratio.

Flow Ratio

The flow ratio estimates the ability of less-liquid current assets to pay down the current liabilities on which a company typically doesn't pay interest. The formula for calculating the flow ratio is:

(Current assets − (Cash + Accounts receivable)) /
(Current liabilities − Short-term debt) = Flow ratio

Using the information in **TABLE B-1**, we can calculate a flow ratio for this company as follows:

(316,419 − (93,378 + 95,689)) / (120,738 − 24,148) = 1.3

Most analysts are looking for a target flow ratio of 1.5 or lower, which represents a good balance between liabilities and less-liquid current assets.

Payable Turnover Ratio

The payable turnover ratio is calculated using this formula:

Cost of goods sold / Average accounts payable = Payable turn

If the company's cost of goods sold is $853,482, the payable turn is calculated as follows:

853,482 / ((96,590 + 107,492) / 2) = 8.36

This company turns over its accounts payables just over eight times a year. How many days of accounts payable the company is carrying is calculated by the days payables ratio (calculated earlier in this appendix).

Quick Ratio (Acid Test)

This calculation is a variation of the current ratio that uses only the amount of current assets that can be quickly converted to cash (typically in the next 90 days) to calculate its relationship to the current liabilities.

The quick ratio is calculated using this formula:

Quick assets / Total current liabilities = Quick ratio

Using the numbers from **TABLE B-1**, the quick ratio is calculated as:

189,067 / 120,738 = 1.57

Most analysts use 1.00 as an indication of liquidity, but this ratio varies by industry.

Receivables Turnover Ratio

This ratio determines the number of times per year the A/R balance should be completely paid off. This ratio is calculated using the following formula:

> Sales / Average accounts receivable balance = Receivable turn

If the company's sales are $1,404,550 and we use the information from **TABLE B-1**, the receivables turnover ratio is calculated as follows:

> 1,404,550 / ((95,689 + 87,800) / 2) = 15.31 turns

The result, 15.31, indicates that the accounts receivables are turning over 15 times per year, or on average more than once per month. To calculate the number of days outstanding, use the days receivable ratio (see above).

Working Capital

To calculate a company's working capital, use the following formula:

> Current assets − Current liabilities = Working capital

For example, using the numbers from **TABLE B-1**, the working capital for this company in 2002 is calculated as:

> 316,419 − 120,738 = 195,681

This company has $195,681 in working capital. Working capital is also referred to as net current assets.

Working Capital Ratio

This ratio, which is a liquidity ratio, shows a company's working capital as a percentage of its total assets. The working capital ratio is calculated using the following formula:

Working capital / Total assets = Working capital ratio

Using the working capital figure we calculated above, we can compute the working capital ratio for this company as follows:

195,681 / 526,360 = 0.37

A working capital ratio of less than 0.25 may be an indication of low or insufficient liquidity.

Income Statement Ratios

The ratios and formulas in this section relate to the income statement. The example given for each ratio draws on the information in **TABLE B-2**, unless otherwise stated.

TABLE B-2: PIES LIKE MOM'S, INC.
2002 INCOME STATEMENT

Pies Like Mom's, Inc.
Income Statement for the Year Ending 12/31/2002

Revenues	
Wholesale sales	$1,707,095
Retail sales	$96,175
Gross revenues	$1,803,270
Cost of sales	
Food costs	$1,315,250
Other direct costs	$39,889
Total cost of sales	$1,355,139
Gross profit	$448,131
Operating expenses	
Selling and administrative expenses	$7,978

Depreciation	$36,872
Total operating expenses	$44,850
Operating income	$403,281
Interest expense	$13,500
Income before taxes	$389,781
Income taxes	$77,956
Net income	$311,825

Contribution Margin

Frequently used to measure the efficiency of manufacturing firms, contribution margin measures the relationship of sales to variable costs. The ratio is expressed as the percentage of revenue remaining after total variable costs are subtracted. With real financial statements for real manufacturing companies, total variable costs may be included as a footnote to the income statement or within the general notes to the financial statements, and may not equal the amount listed as cost of goods sold. In this example, cost of goods sold is used for the total variable costs.

The formula for calculating contribution margin in dollars is:

Sales revenue – Variable costs = Contribution margin

Using the information in **TABLE B-2**, the contribution margin is calculated as follows:

1,803,270 – 1,355,139 = 448,131

Contribution Margin Ratio

The contribution margin ratio converts the contribution margin amount into a ratio that represents the percentage of sales represented by the contribution margin. It is calculated as follows:

Contribution margin / Sales revenue = Contribution margin ratio

Using the information from **TABLE B-2**, the contribution margin ratio is calculated as:

$$448,131 / 1,803,270 = 0.25$$

A contribution margin ratio of 0.25 indicates that 25 cents of every sales dollar is available to cover overhead.

Earnings Growth Ratio

When looking at numbers like EPS, you must also consider the growth rates of the companies (and their industries) being considered. The EPS growth rate calculation is calculated using the following formula:

$$\text{(Year 2 earnings - Year 1 earnings) / Year 1 earnings} \times 100 = \text{Growth ratio}$$

We find on its Web site that Pies Like Mom's, Inc. (PLM) had an EPS ratio for 2001 of $0.23. Its 2002 EPS was $0.31 (calculated in the following example), so its earnings growth rate is calculated as follows:

$$(0.31 - 0.23) / 0.23 \times 100 = 34.78$$

So, PLM's growth rate for the years 2001/2002 is 34.78%.

Earning per Share Ratio

The earnings per share (EPS) ratio is calculated by dividing a company's earnings (net income) by the number of outstanding shares (the number of shares a company has issued). Using the information provided in **TABLE B-3** and assuming that Pies Like Mom's, Inc. (PLM) currently has 1,000,000 shares outstanding, its earnings per share amount is calculated as follows:

$$\text{Net income / Shares outstanding} = \text{EPS}$$

$$\$311,825 / 1,000,000 = \$0.31$$

The above calculation tells us that at the end of 2002, PLM had an EPS ratio of $0.31.

Gross Profit

Gross profit is the net of the sales and the cost of goods sold for a period. This number is important because it is a first indication of whether a company is selling enough of its products or services to cover its product costs. Gross profit is calculated as follows:

Revenues – Cost of sales = Gross income

Using the information in **TABLE B-2**, the gross profit is calculated as:

1,803,270 – 1,355,139 = 448,131

Gross Margin Ratio

The gross margin profitability ratio can be used to analyze a company's efficiency in producing and distributing its products or services. Gross margin is calculated as gross profit divided by net revenues, using the following formula:

Gross profit / Revenues = Gross margin ratio

Using the sales and cost of sales amounts from **TABLE B-2**, the gross margin ratio is calculated as:

448,131 / 1,803,270 = 0.25

A gross margin percentage of 0.25 indicates that gross profit is 25% of revenues.

Interest Coverage Ratio

The interest coverage ratio measures a company's ability to meet its interest-bearing debt obligations with its regular earnings. The interest coverage ratio is calculated using the following formula:

Operating income / Interest expense = Interest coverage ratio

Using the information from **TABLE B-2**, the company's interest coverage ratio is calculated as:

403,281 / 13,500 = 29.87

An interest coverage ratio of less than 2.0 normally indicates that earnings are not sufficiently high enough to provide coverage for interest payments on interest-bearing debt. Clearly, this company is earning enough to cover its interest obligations.

Net Income

Net income, which is also called net profit or net earnings, reflects the profits generated by a company after its interest and income tax expenses are deducted from its operational income. Net income is calculated as follows:

Operating income – (Interest + income tax) = Net income

A positive net income indicates the company made a net profit from its overall operations, including any interest payments or taxes it paid during the period.

Using the information in **TABLE B-2**, net income is calculated as:

403,281 – (13,500 + 77,956) = 311,825

Net Margin Ratio

Another profitability ratio is net margin, which measures the overall profitability of a business. The net margin ratio is calculated using the following formula:

Net profit / Revenues = Net margin

The net margin ratio states net profit as a percentage of net revenues. From the information in **TABLE B-2**, the net margin calculation is:

$$311,825 / 1,803,270 = 0.17$$

The higher a company's net margin ratio is in comparison to its industry average indicates how competitive the company is in the marketplace.

Operating Income

A company's operating income is an indication of its earning power from its product or service operations. Operating income is calculated as follows:

Gross profit – Operating expenses = Operating income

Operating expense includes administrative expenses, research and development expenses, depreciation, and the like. Using information from **TABLE B-2**, the operating income is calculated as:

$$448,131 - 44,850 = 403,281$$

Operating Margin

A company's operating margin ratio indicates the quality of its operations, in terms of its operating efficiency.

The operating margin ratio is calculated using the following formula:

Operating income / Net sales = Operating margin

Using the information from **TABLE B-2**, the operating margin is calculated as follows:

$$403,281 / 1,803,270 = 0.22$$

The 2002 operating margin ratio for PLM is 22%, which should be compared to its industry average to determine whether the result is good or bad. Generally speaking, though, an operating margin greater than 20% is considered good for a product-oriented business.

Price to Earnings Ratio

The price to earnings (P/E) ratio compares a company's current share price to its earnings per share (EPS). The P/E ratio is calculated using the following formula:

> Stock price / EPS = Price to earnings ratio

In a previous example, we calculated PLM's EPS to be $0.31 (based on the information in **TABLE B-2**). If PLM's current stock price is $3.00, its P/E ratio is 9.7, which is calculated as follows:

> 3.00 / 0.31 = 9.7

Whether a P/E ratio of 9.7, which would also be stated as 9x (9 times), is good or bad requires comparison to either a prior period's P/E ratio or comparison to other firms in the same industry.

Price/Earnings to Growth Ratio

The price/earnings to growth (PEG) ratio is an indicator ratio used to identify stocks with good growth potential. PEG is calculated as follows:

> P/E ratio / Projected growth rate = Price / earnings to growth ratio

Using PLM's P/E ratio (calculated above) and its growth rate of 34.78 (calculated earlier in this appendix) we can calculate the 2002 PEG as:

> 9.7 / 34.78 = 0.28

Price to Book Value Ratio

The price to book value (P/BV) ratio is used to compare a company's share price to the company's book value per share. The P/BV ratio is calculated using the following formula:

> Share price / Book value per share = Price to book value ratio

In 2002 PLM had a book value of $1,261,825, its current share price is $3.00, and it has 1,000,000 shares outstanding. For 2002, PLM's P/BV ratio of 2.38 is determined as follows:

> 3.00 / (1,261,825 / 1,000,000) = 2.38

Price to Sales Ratio

The price to sales (P/S) ratio is often used to replace the P/E ratio when a company has negative income. The P/S ratio is calculated as follows:

> Share price / Sales per share = Price to sales ratio

If PLM's current stock price is $3.00 per share and its sales per share for 2002 is 1.80 (based on the information in **TABLE B-2**), PLM's P/S ratio is calculated as follows:

> 3.00 / 1.80 = 1.67

Return on Assets Ratio

How well a company is able to use its assets to generate earnings from its operations is indicated by its return on assets (ROA) ratio. This ratio is calculated using the following formula:

> Net income / Total assets = Return on assets

Using the numbers from **TABLE B-2** and PLM's total assets of $2,500,000, the return on assets ratio is calculated as follows:

> 311,825 / 2,500,000 = 0.12

In other words, the company is generating about $0.12 of net income with each dollar of total assets.

Return on Equity Ratio

The return on equity (ROE) ratio measures earnings made possible through investment in a company. The ROE ratio is calculated using the following formula:

Net income / Shareholders' equity = Return on equity

Using the information in **TABLE B-2** and PLM's 2002 equity of $1,261,825, the ROE is calculated as follows:

311,825 / 1,261,825 = .25

A ROE ratio of .25 indicates that for each dollar of investment capital, the company is able to generate $0.25 of earnings.

Return on Sales Ratio

The return on sales (ROS) ratio measures how much net income is generated by each dollar of sales. ROS is calculated using the following formula:

Net income / Revenues = Return on sales

Using the information from the income statement in **TABLE B-2**, ROS is calculated as follows:

311,825 / 1,803,270 = 0.17

An ROS ratio of 0.17 indicates the company is netting about 17% profit on sales.

Times Interest Earned Ratio

The times interest earned (TIE) ratio, which is also called the interest coverage ratio, indicates the relationship between a company's earnings before interest and taxes (EBIT) and the amount of interest the company paid to outside creditors, lenders, and bondholders. It is used as an indication of a company's solvency. (EBIT may be called operating income.)

The TIE ratio is calculated as follows:

EBIT / Interest payments = Times interest earned ratio

Using the information from **TABLE B-2**, the TIE ratio is calculated as:

403,281 / 13,500 = 29.9

A TIE ratio above one indicates the business has sufficient earnings to cover its interest payments.

Cash Flow Ratios

Cash flow has become a very important part of ratio and financial analysis. New ratios and formulas continue to be developed to measure the cash flow performance of a company. This section contains most of the primary and commonly used cash flow ratios and formulas. The cash flows statement shown in **TABLE B-3** was prepared using the indirect method. (For a full discussion of this method, see Chapter 6.)

TABLE B-3: A CASH FLOWS STATEMENT

Ronprico Enterprises, Inc.
Cash Flows Statement for the Year Ending 12/31/02

Cash Flow from Operating Activities

Net income	$30,903
Depreciation expense	$3,133
Increase in accounts receivable	$(9,225)
Decrease in inventory	$15,357
Decrease in prepaid expenses	$2,500

TABLE B-3: A CASH FLOWS
STATEMENT (CONTINUED)

Increase in accounts payable	$5,453
Increase in accrued expenses	$4,428
Decrease in interest payable	$(4,725)
Decrease in income taxes payable	$(2,500)
Total cash flow from operating activities	$45,324

Cash Flow from Investing

Purchase of property and equipment	$(12,300)
Total cash flow from investing	$(12,300)

Cash Flow from Financing

Increase in long-term debt	$22,451
Issuance of capital stock	$26,638
Dividend payments	$(4,000)
Total cash flow from financing	$45,089
Net increase in cash	$78,113
Cash at beginning of year	$120,000
Cash at end of year	$198,113

Capital Expenditure Ratio

The capital expenditure (CE) ratio measures the cash flow available for future investment and for payments on existing debt. This ratio is calculated using the following formula:

(Cash flow from operations – Dividends) / Fixed asset payments = Capital expenditure ratio

Using the information from **TABLE B-3**, the company's CE ratio is calculated as follows:

$$(45{,}324 - 4{,}000) / 12{,}300 = 3.36$$

A CE ratio of greater than 1.0 indicates that a company is able to cover its capital investments with its operating cash flows, with money still available to pay its debts.

Cash Flow Growth Ratio

An indicator of financial strength is cash flow growth, or a positive rate of change in cash flow from year to year. Cash flow growth is calculated using the following formula, where Y2 represents the cash flow from the current or latest period and Y1 represents the cash flow from the earlier or previous period:

(Y2 cash flow – Y1 cash flow) / Y1 cash flow = Cash flow growth ratio

If Ronprico Enterprises experienced $70,000 of cash flow in a prior year and $78,113 in the current year (as per **TABLE B-3**), the cash flow growth ratio is calculated as follows:

$$(78{,}113 - 70{,}000) / 70{,}000 = 0.12 \text{ or } 12\%$$

The benchmark for the cash flow growth ratio varies widely from industry to industy.

Cash Flow per Share Ratio

The cash flow per share (CFPS) ratio is an indicator of a company's financial strength and is calculated using the following formula:

Cash flows from operations / Shares outstanding = Cash flow per share

If Ronprico has 100,000 shares outstanding, its cash flow per share is calculated as:

$$78{,}113 / 100{,}000 = 0.78$$

How good or bad the CFPS may be depends on the average for

its industry and the investor's perception when comparing this ratio to other companies.

Cash Interest Coverage Ratio

The cash interest coverage (CIC) ratio measures how well cash flows are able to cover cash payments made for interest on interest-bearing debt. The CIC ratio is calculated using the following formula:

(Cash flows from operations + Interest payments + Taxes payments) / Interest payments = Cash interest coverage ratio

Ronprico Enterprises's cash flows statement shows cash flows from operations of $45,324, including interest payments of $4,725 and income tax payments of $2,500. Its CIC ratio is calculated as follows:

(45,324 + 4,725 + 2,500) / 4,725 = 11.12

A CIC ratio of 11.12 indicates the company is generating over 10 times as much cash as it requires to pay its interest obligations. Obviously, the lower this ratio is for a company, the more you need to be concerned about its ability to meet its interest-bearing debt obligations.

Cash to Current Debt Coverage Ratio

The cash to current debt coverage ratio (CCD), also called the cash current debt coverage ratio (CDC), is used to measure a company's ability to repay its current debt through its cash flows from operations. The CCD ratio is calculated using the following formula:

(Cash flows from operations – Cash dividends) / Current debt = Cash to current debt coverage ratio

Using the information from **TABLE B-3** and the additional information that this company has current interest-bearing liabilities of $25,000, its CCD ratio is calculated as:

$$(45,324 - 4,000) / 25,000 = 1.65$$

A CCD ratio of greater than 1.0 indicates the company's operating activities are generating sufficient cash flow to cover its current liabilities.

Debt to Cash Flow Ratio

The debt to cash flow (DCF) ratio measures the company's overall cash flow and its ability to cover all of the company's debt (current and long-term). Debt to cash flow ratio is calculated using the following formula:

Total debt / Total cash flows = Debt to cash flow ratio

For example, if Ronprico Enterprises currently has a total of current and long-term debt of $300,000, its DCF ratio is calculated as follows:

$$300,000 / 78,113 = 3.84$$

A DCF ratio of 1.0 or lower indicates that a company's debt can be considered current debt because it could be paid off within one year using current cash flows (even though there is no requirement to do so).

Free Cash Flow

Free cash is the dollar amount a business could use for expansion and growth after all of its obligations are met. Free cash is calculated using the following formula:

Operating cash flow – Dividends – Net capital expenditures =
Free cash flow

Based on **TABLE B-3**, free cash flow is calculated as follows:

$$45,324 - 4,000 - 12,300 = 29,024$$

Free Cash Flow per Share Ratio

A company's free cash flow per share ratio is calculated using the following formula:

Free cash flow / Shares outstanding = Free cash flow per share ratio

If the company in **TABLE B-3** has 100,000 shares outstanding, its free cash flow per share ratio is 0.29, which is calculated as follows:

29,024 / 100,000 = .29

A free cash flow per share ratio of 0.29 shows that the company has 29 cents per share that can be used to grow the company—or to pay out extra dividends.

Operating Cash Flow Ratio

The operating cash flow (OCF) ratio is a measure of a company's ability to cover its current liabilities through its cash flow from operations. The OCF ratio is calculated using the following formula:

Cash flows from operations / Current liabilities =
Operating cash flow ratio

Using the information in **TABLE B-3** and using $39,235 for its total current liabilities, the OCF ratio for this company is calculated as:

45,324 / 39,235 = 1.16

An OCF ratio of 1.0 or more indicates the company is generating sufficient cash flows from operations to pay its current debts.

Price to Cash Flow Ratio

The price to cash flow ratio is calculated using the following formula:

Current share price / Operating cash flow per share =
Price to cash flow ratio

For example, if Ronprico's stock is currently trading at $4.25 and its operating cash flow per share is .45 (calculated by dividing net operating cash flow by number of shares outstanding), its price to cash flow ratio is calculated as follows:

$$4.25 / 0.45 = 9.44$$

A higher price to cash flow ratio can indicate a stock that is overvalued against the cash flows being generated by a company.

Price to Free Cash Flow Ratio

The price to free cash flow ratio measures the relative value of a company's stock in terms of the company's free cash flow. This ratio is calculated using the following formula:

Current share price / Free cash flow per share =
Price to free cash flow ratio

The current share price of Ronprico Enterprises is $4.25 and its free cash flow per share is $0.29 (calculated previously in this section). With that information, its price to free cash flow ratio is 14.65, which is calculated as follows:

$$4.25 / .29 = 14.65$$

As with the price to cash flow ratio, a higher result can indicate that a corporation's stock is overvalued in terms of free cash flow produced.

Index

Income statement ratios, *(continued)*
  EBITDA, 88–90
  gross margin, 81–82, 83, 177
  net margin ratio, 84–85,
    178–79
  operating margin, 83–84,
    179–80
  price/earnings to growth (PEG)
    ratio, 94, 180
  price to book value (P/BV)
    ratio, 95, 180–81
  price to earnings growth ratio,
    92–93
  price to earnings (P/E) ratio,
    91–92, 141–42, 180
  price to sales (P/S) ratio, 94–95,
    181
  profitability ratios, 81–90
  ROA ratio, 85–86, 181
  ROE/ROI ratio, 87, 182
  ROS ratio, 87–88, 182
  share to earnings ratios, 90–95
  times interest earned (TIE)
    ratio, 80–81, 182–83
Income statements, 63–77
  components, 16–20
  comprehensive income, 20
  cost of sales, 18, 67–68
  defined, 16
  gross profit, 18, 68–69, 177
  indirect expenses, 19–20, 74,
    75
  net income, 20, 75, 178
  operating expenses, 16, 17, 18,
    69, 107–8
  operating income, 19, 74, 179
  purpose, 63–64
  revenues, 17, 66
  samples, 16–17, 65, 83, 86
  See also Income statement
    ratios

Income taxes
  expenses, 19, 20, 75
  payable, 39
Indirect expenses, 19–20
  interest, 19, 20, 74
  taxes, 19, 20, 75
Information sources, 138–39
Intangible assets, 12, 37–38
Interest coverage ratio, 177–78
Interest expense, 19, 20, 74
Inventory
  accounting methods, 35–37
  average, 58
  as cash flow indicator, 117
  lower of cost or market, 36–37
  overview, 34
  shrinkage, 68
  turnover ratio, 57–58
  valuation, 36–37, 67–68, 137
  writing down value, 36–37, 68
Investing
  effective cash flow and, 117
  financial analysts and, 136,
    141–42
  financial statement focus, 136
  free cash flow and, 128
  fundamental analysis and,
    141–42
  high-tech companies and,
    132–34
  technical analysis and, 142
  Web sites, 92, 128, 130
Investing activity cash flows, 23,
  110–11
Investments, short-term, 34

L

Labor leaders, 136
Latest twelve months (LTM)
  earnings, 91
Lenders. *See* Bankers

About the Author

Ron Price is an accomplished author of technical books. He holds an M.B.A. as well as a variety of technical certifications. Mr. Price also has extensive experience as a managing consultant with an international auditing firm.